Midland Ontario Book 2 in Colour Photos, Saving Our History One Photo at a Time

Photography
by Barbara Raué
2016

Series Name: Cruising Ontario

Book 151: Midland Book 2

Cover photo: 657 Hugel Avenue, Page 32

Series Name: Cruising Ontario
Saving Our History One Photo at a Time
in colour photos

Books Available in Alphabetical Order:
Aberfoyle, Acton, Alton, Amherstburg, Ancaster, Arthur, Aylmer, Ayr, Bloomingdale, Brantford, Burlington, Caledon, Caledonia, Cambridge, Clifford, Conestogo, Delhi, Dorchester to Aylmer, Drayton, Drumbo, Dundas, Eden Mills, Elmira, Elora, Essex, Fergus, Guelph, Hagersville, Hamilton, Hanover, Harriston, Hespeler, Jarvis, Kingston, Kingsville, Kitchener, Linwood, Listowel, London, Lucknow, Mono, Mount Forest, Neustadt, New Hamburg, Niagara-on-the-Lake, Oakville, Orangeville, Orillia, Owen Sound, Palmerston, Peterborough, Petrolia, Port Elgin, Preston, Rockwood, Sarnia, Seaforth, Sheffield, Shelburne, Simcoe, Southampton, St. Jacobs, St. Marys, St. Thomas, Stoney Creek, Stratford, Thamesford, Tillsonburg, Waterdown, Waterford, Waterloo, Welland, Wellesley, Windsor, Wingham, Woodstock

Other Books by Barbara Raue

Coins of Gold

Arrows, Indians and Love

The Life and Times of Barbara
Volume 1: Inventions That Have Enhanced My Life
Volume 2: Entertainment That I Have Enjoyed
Volume 3: East Coast Trips
Volume 4: Olympics Have Always Intrigued Me
Volume 5: Wonders of the World
Volume 6: Caribbean Cruises We Have Enjoyed
Volume 7: Animals
Volume 8: Storms and Other Major Disasters in My Lifetime
Volume 9: Wars, Terrorist Attacks and Major Disasters

The Cromwell Family Book

Laura Secord Discovered

Daddy Where Are You?

Montana Series
Book 1: Montana Dream
Book 2: Life on the Montana Frontier
Book 3: Montana to Boston and Back

Visit Barbara's website to view all of her books
http://barbararaue.ca

Table of Contents

Midland is located on the southern end of Georgian Bay's 30,000 Islands about ninety miles north of Toronto.

In 1871 a group of the principal shareholders of the Midland Railway, headed by Adolph Hugel, chose this location as the northern terminus of their line which they ran from Port Hope to Beaverton. The town site was surveyed in 1872-73. The railway line was completed in 1879 and soon attracted settlers to the area. The new community, Midland, achieved its early growth through shipping and the lumber and grain trade.

John Dollar established the Ontario Lumber Company in 1875. The success of Dollar's operations led to the construction of a series of "mill houses" just outside the eastern limits of the community known as "Dollar Town". This section was annexed by the town in 1904. Dollar also erected the first board sidewalk in Midland, running from his Hugel Avenue home eastward to Knox Presbyterian Church. The Dollar family left Midland in 1890.

The Dollar House, 657 Hugel Avenue (see Page 30), was later occupied by William Finlayson, lawyer, municipal leader, provincial legislator and cabinet minister. Finlayson entered into a local law practice with W.H. Bennett (later Senator Bennett) in 1897 and later with George S. Dudley. He served as mayor of Midland from 1906-07. Elected to the Ontario legislature as MPP for East Simcoe, Finlayson served from 1923 to 1934 and 1937 to 1939. From 1926 to 1934 he was Minister of Lands and Forests. His interest in the town's municipal affairs was highlighted by his involvement in obtaining the funds necessary for the construction of the Midland Arena Gardens in 1931.

Martyrs' Shrine honors the eight Jesuit priests and their companions who, 350 years ago, lived, worked and died while serving various Native peoples of Canada.

Two-and-a-half-hour cruise through some of the 30,000 islands of Georgian Bay on Miss Midland, a 300 passenger cruise boat

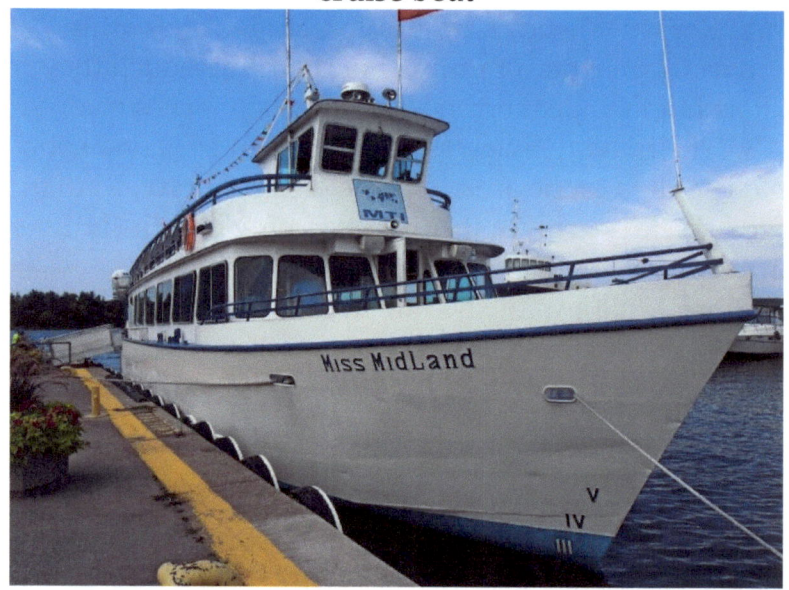

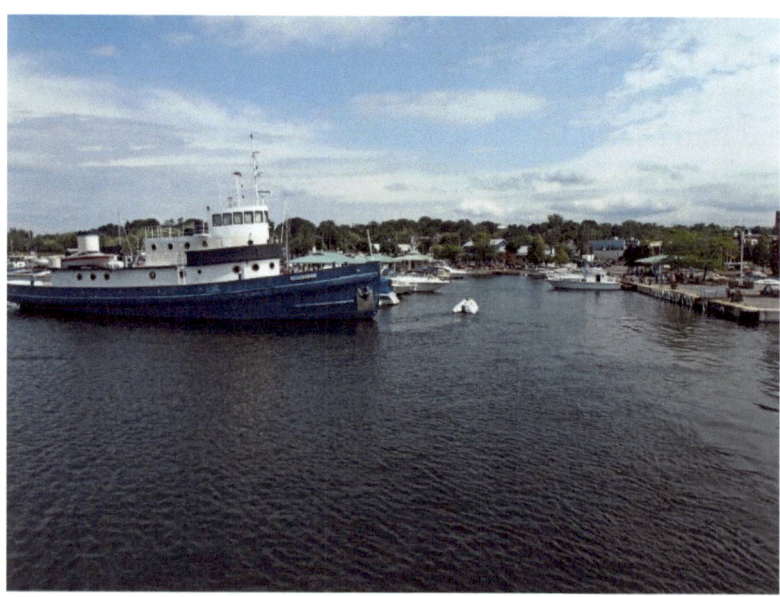

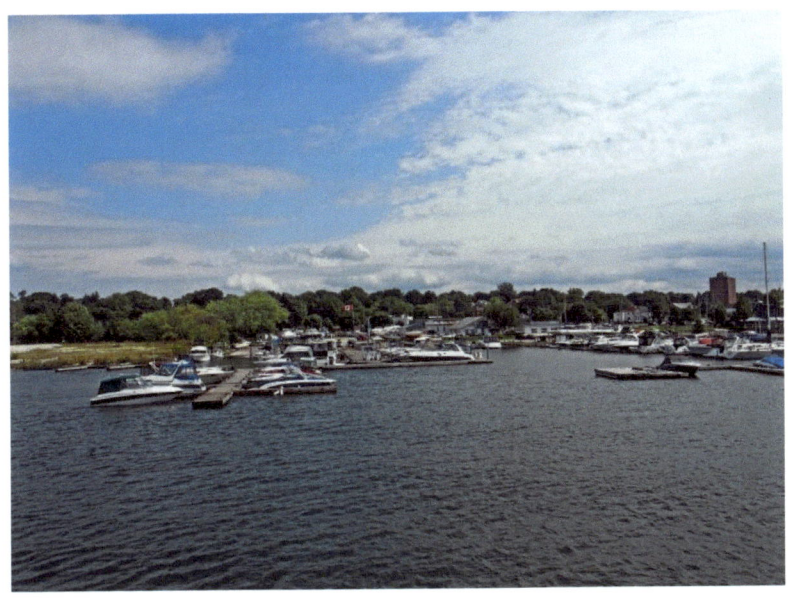

Boats of all sizes on the water, both motor and sail

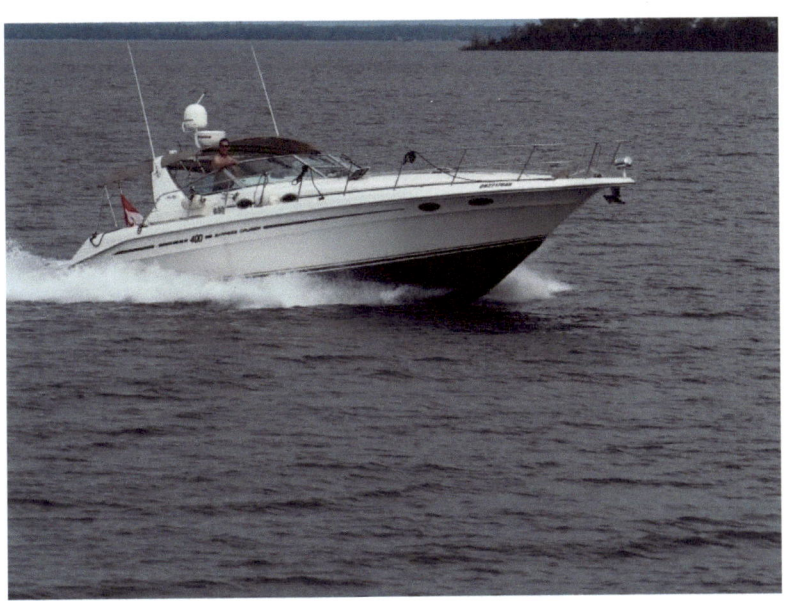

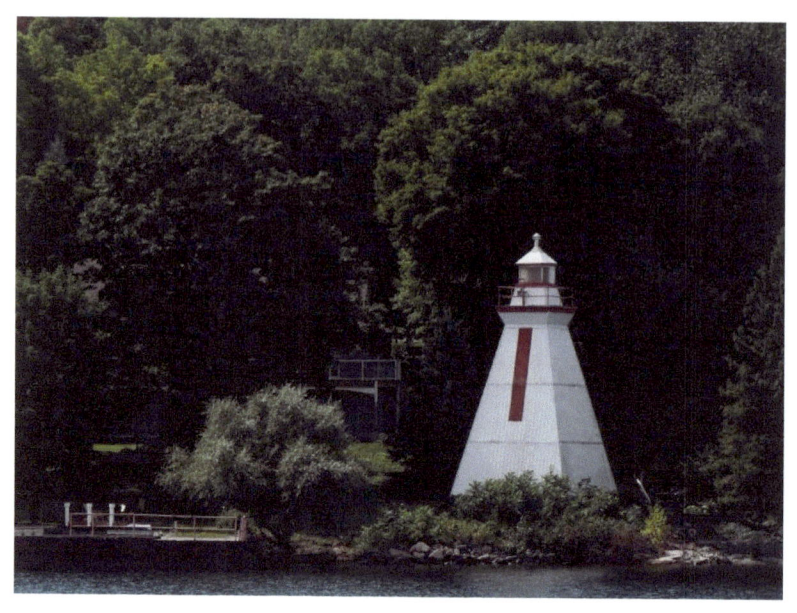

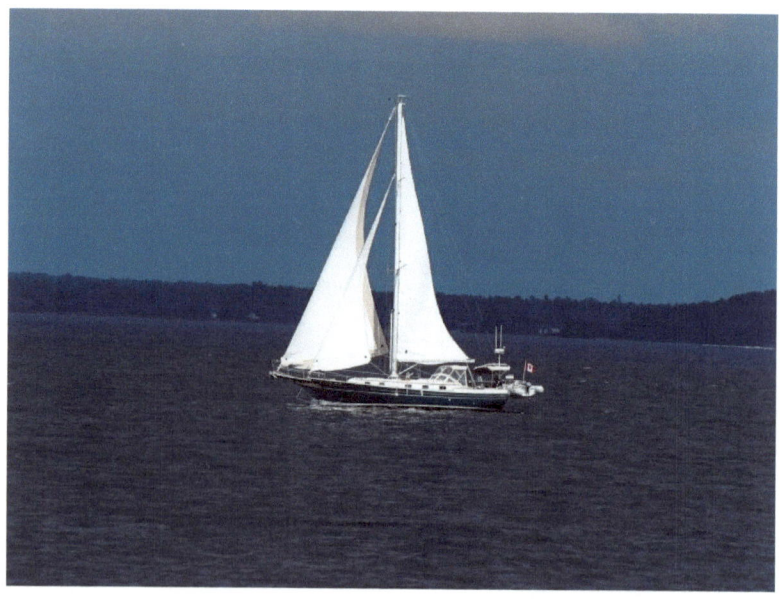

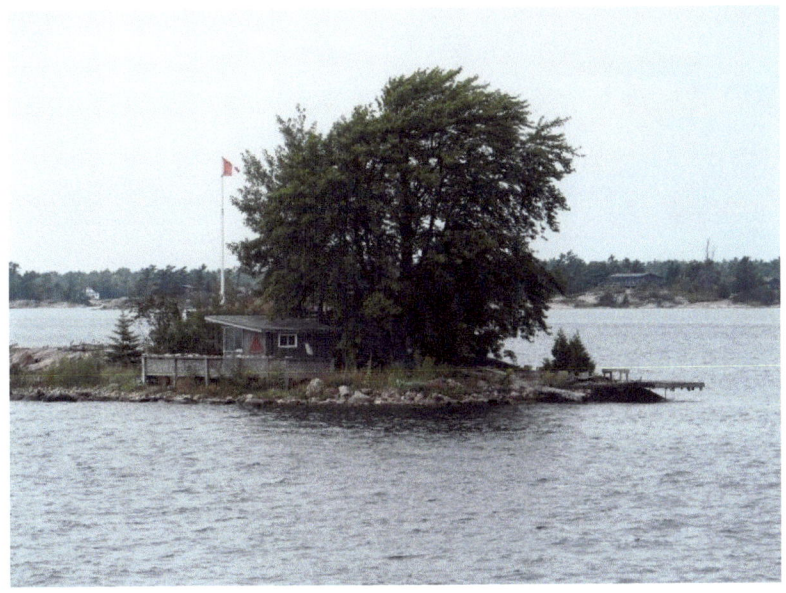

Some of the islands we cruised by were Snake, Present, Beausoleil, Gin, Smooth Islands, Penetang Rock, Tomahawk, Little Beausoleil, Royal, Picnic, Roberts, and Quarry Islands

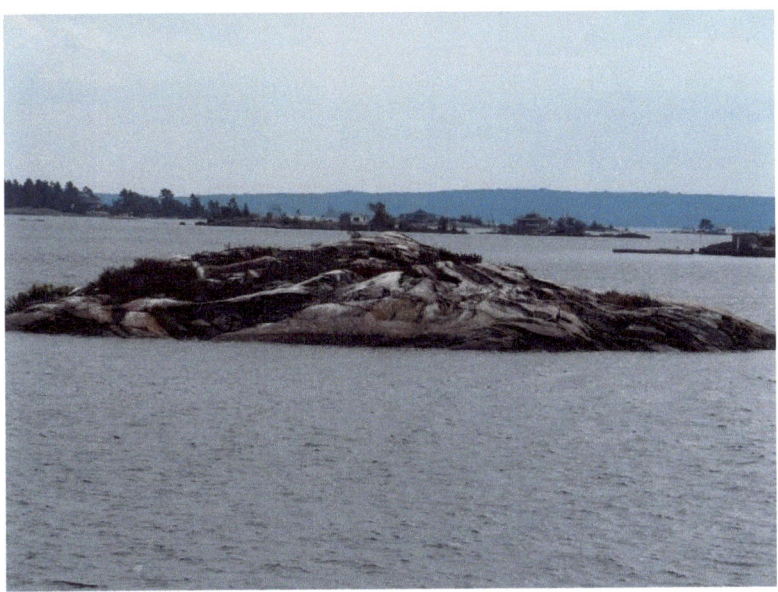

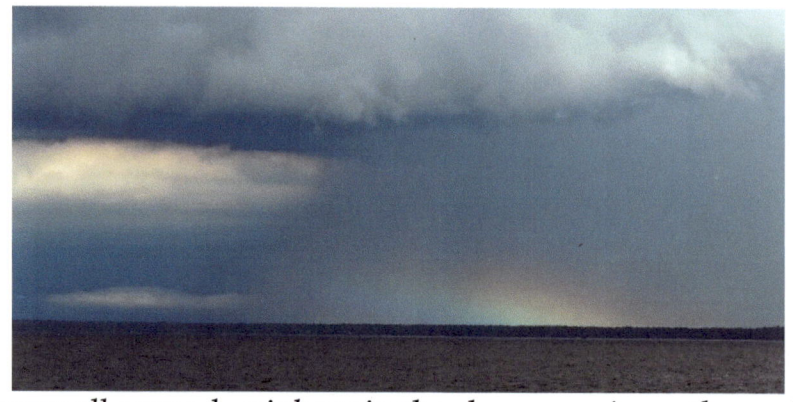

Storms all around, rainbow in the sky – no rain on the cruise ship

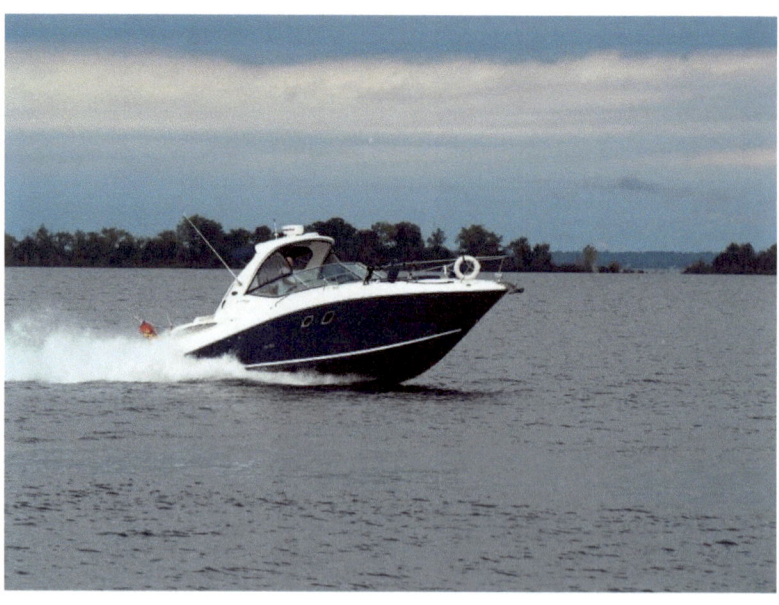

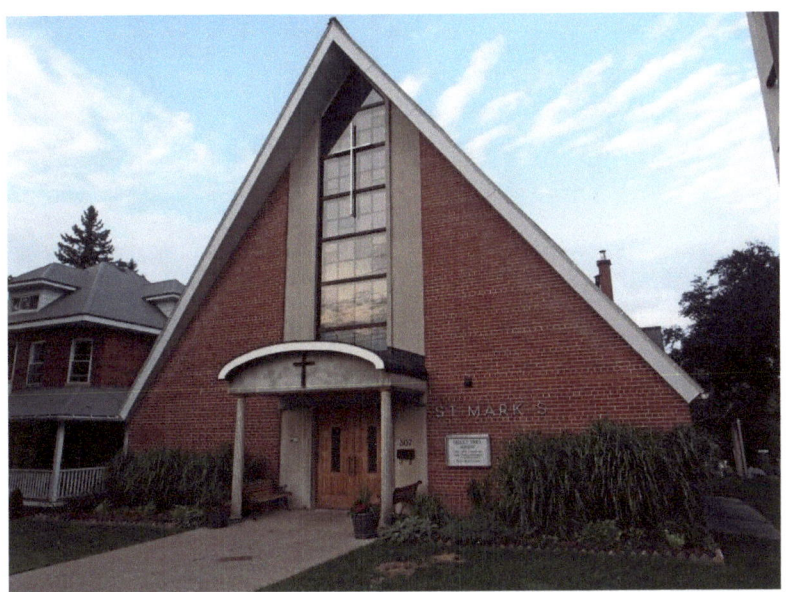

307 Third Street - St. Mark's Anglican Church – 1953 – what is now the front entranceway and belfry as well as second storey gallery were built

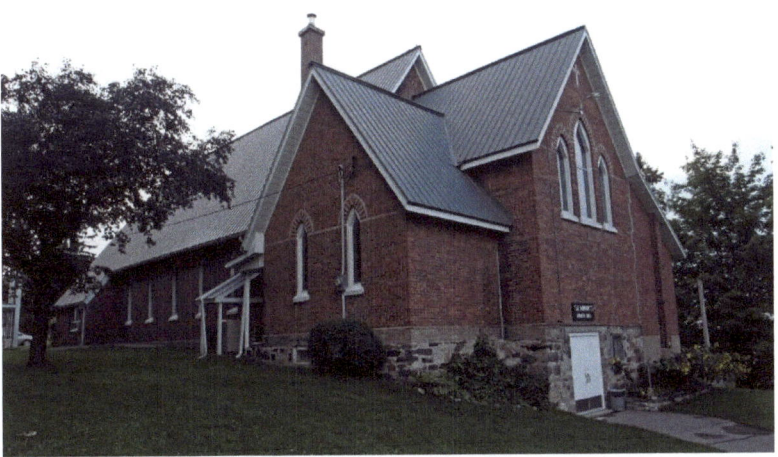

1883 – Gothic Revival style - steep gables on the front façade and bell tower; quatrefoil verge board on the bell tower; simple, pointed lancet windows; and simple dichromatic brick detailing and banding; original stained glassed windows

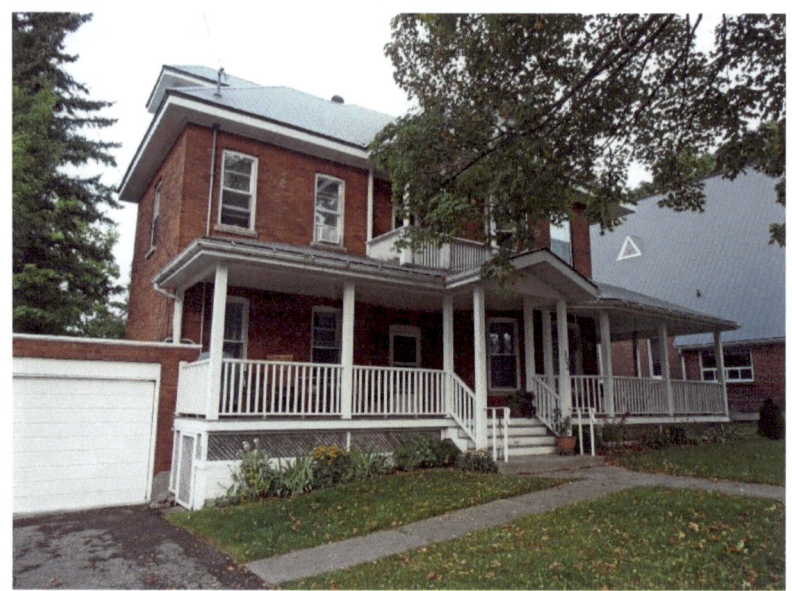

303 Third Street – 1900 - original manse of St. Mark's Anglican Church; 2½ storey home; exterior finished with clapboard, stretcher brick; upper storey door and balcony; truncated medium hipped roof with a hipped dormer; brick voussoirs; open veranda with open railings and wood piers

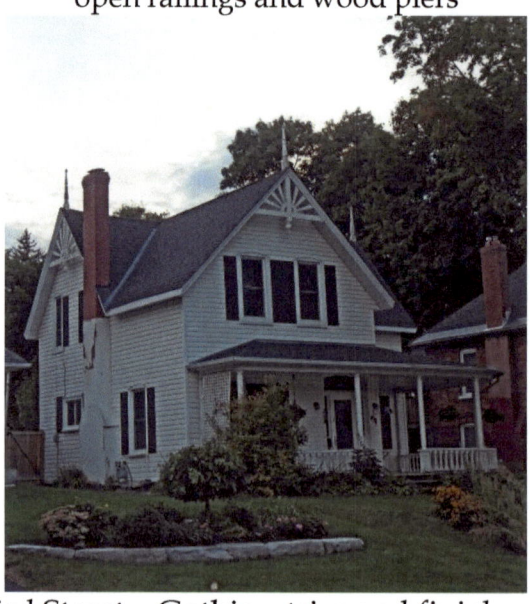

294 Third Street – Gothic – trim and finial on gables

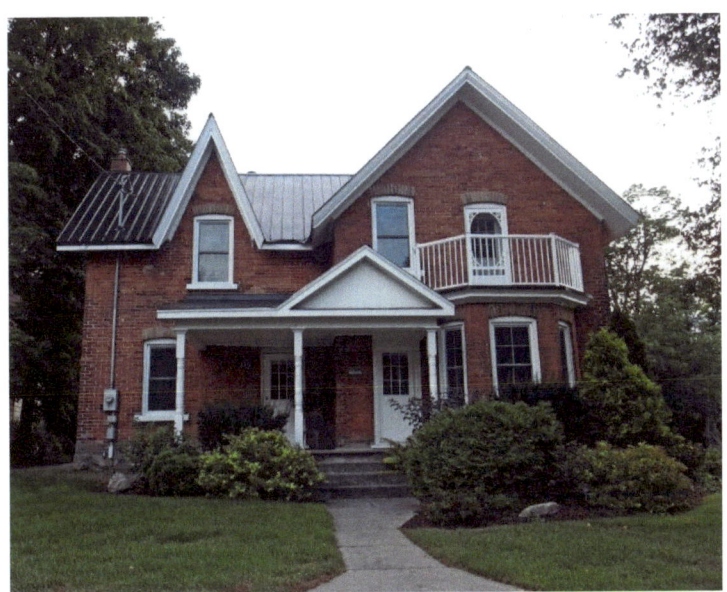

318 Third Street – 1900 – Victorian - irregular layout; medium gabled roof; double gable on façade; fascia and soffit are molded metal; exterior is stretcher brick and vertical plank board; two balconies; brick voussoirs; 4-over-4 window panes; blind transom; open porch with wood posts and pediment

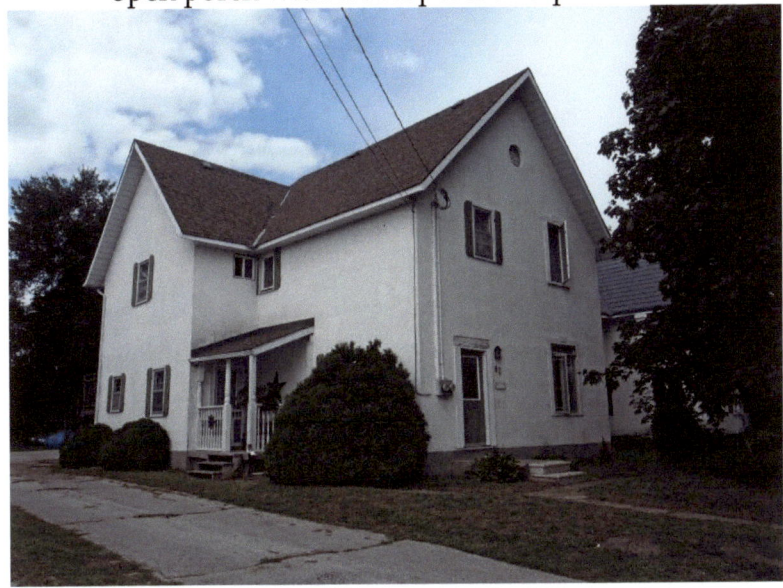

82 Fourth Street - Gothic

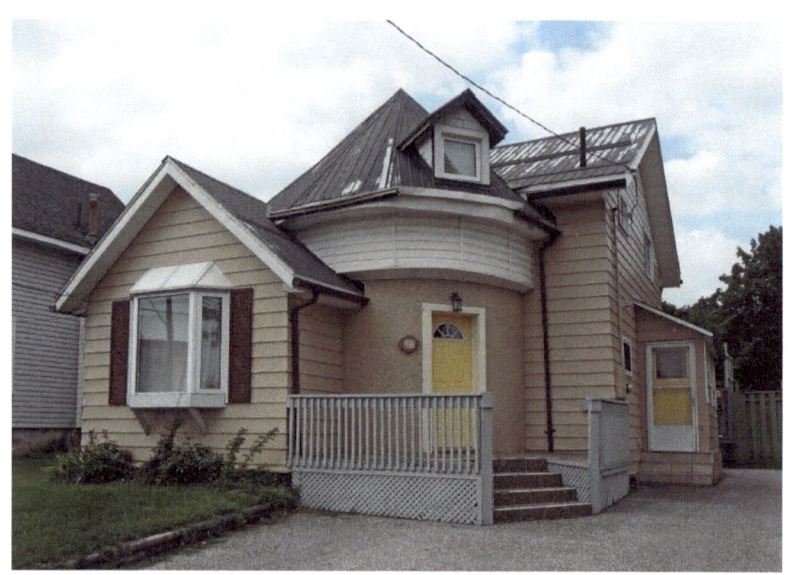

86 Fourth Street – dormer in turret-like structure

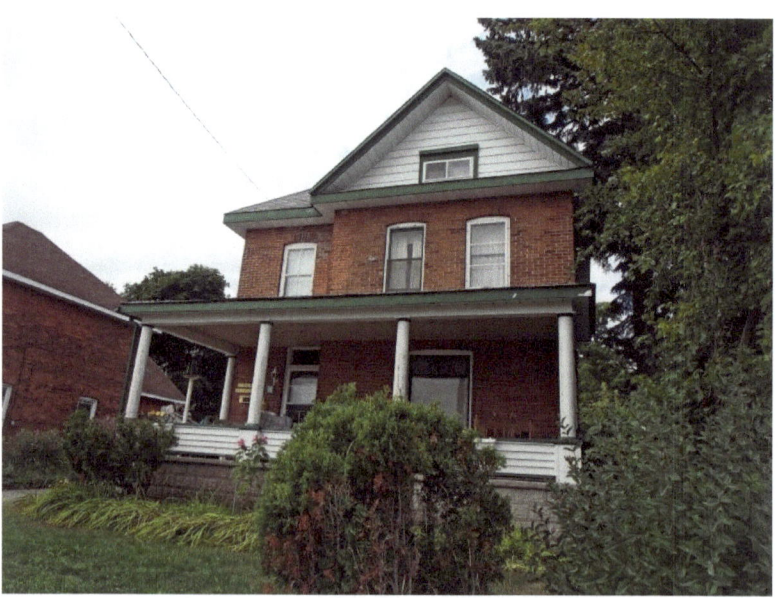

94 Fourth Street - Edwardian

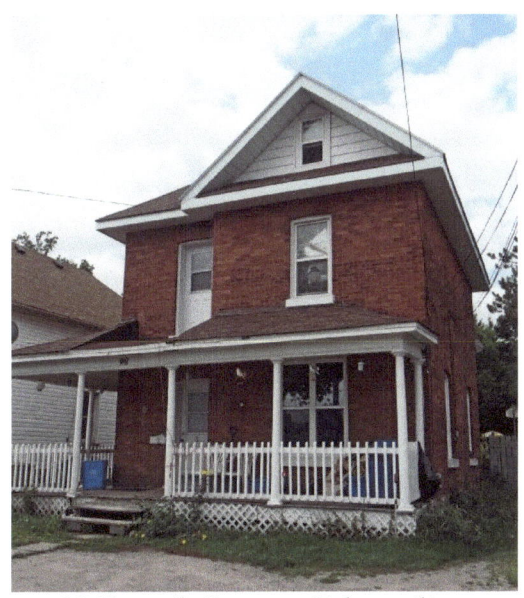

98 Fourth Street - Edwardian

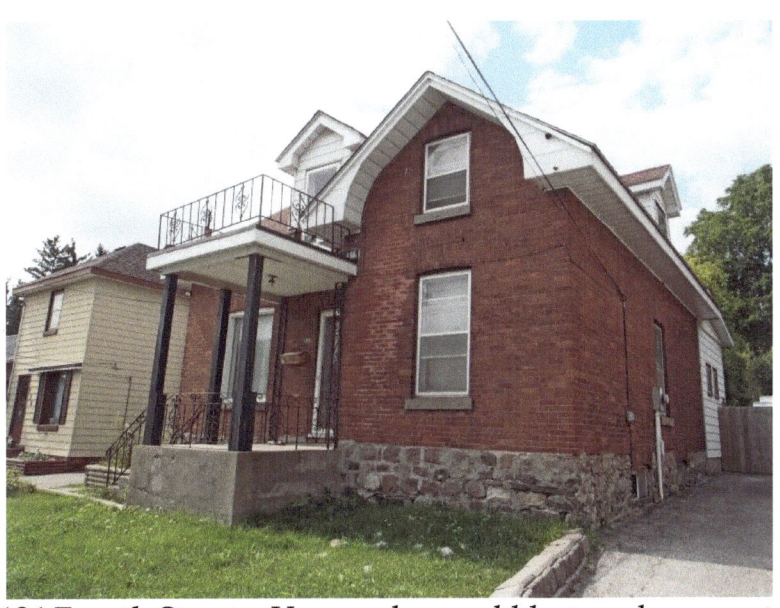

124 Fourth Street – Vernacular – cobblestone basement,
dormers, second floor balcony above porch

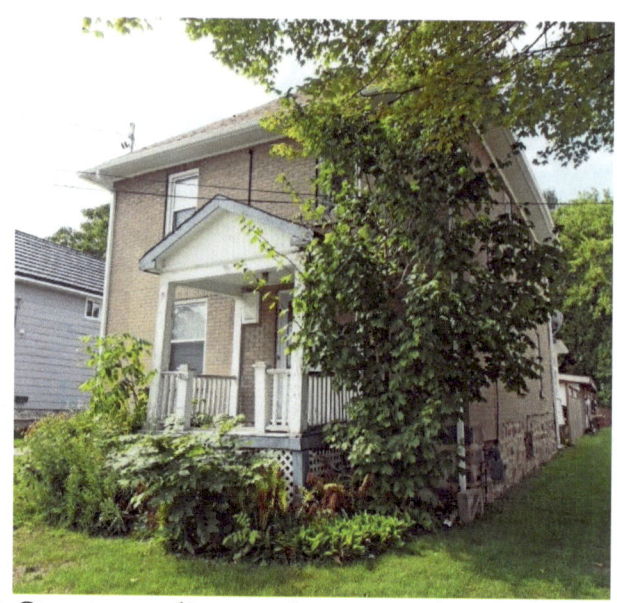

Fourth Street – pediment above porch which has square pillars and open railings

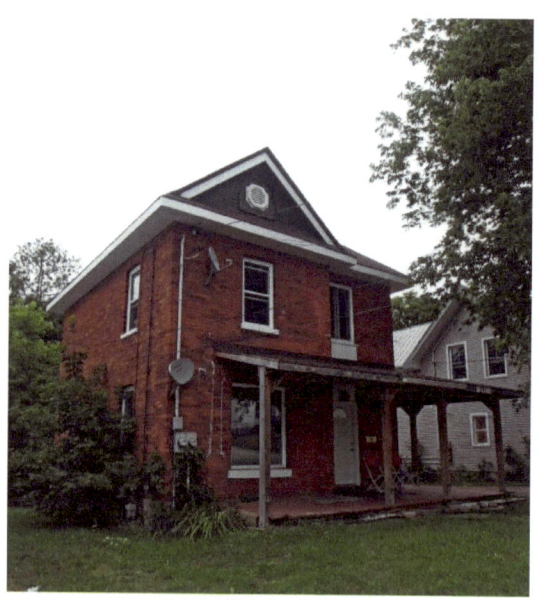

191 Fifth Street

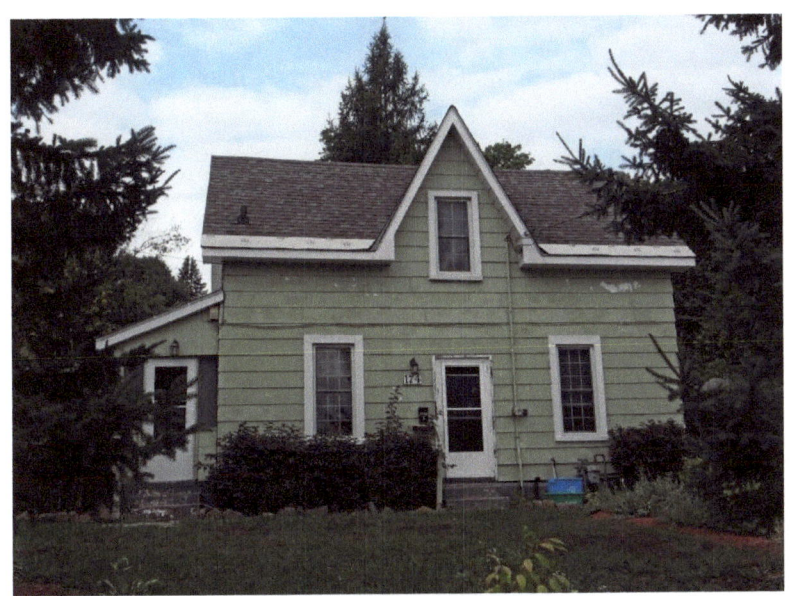

174 Fifth Street - Gothic

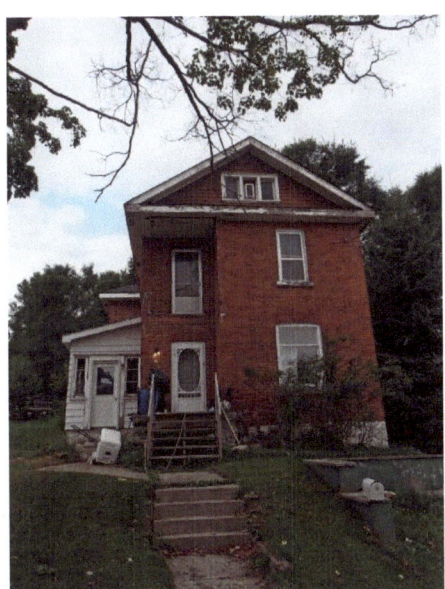

162 Fifth Street - Edwardian

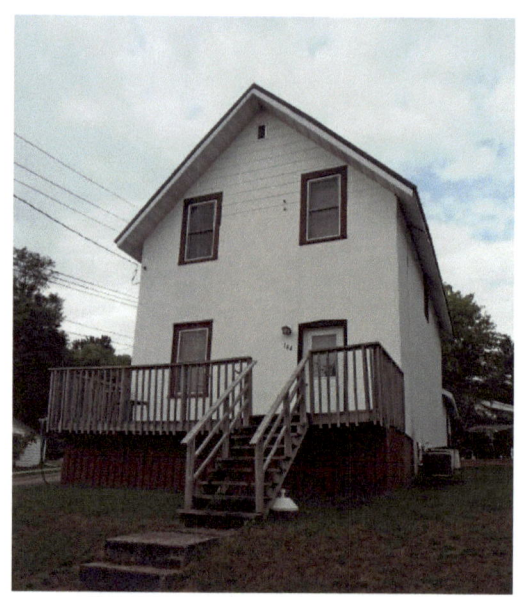

144 Fifth Street - Gothic

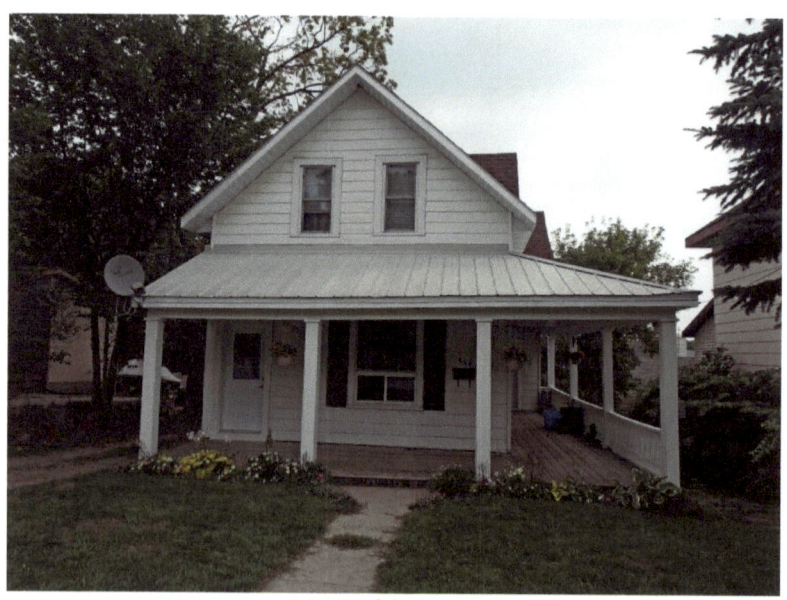

141 Fifth Street

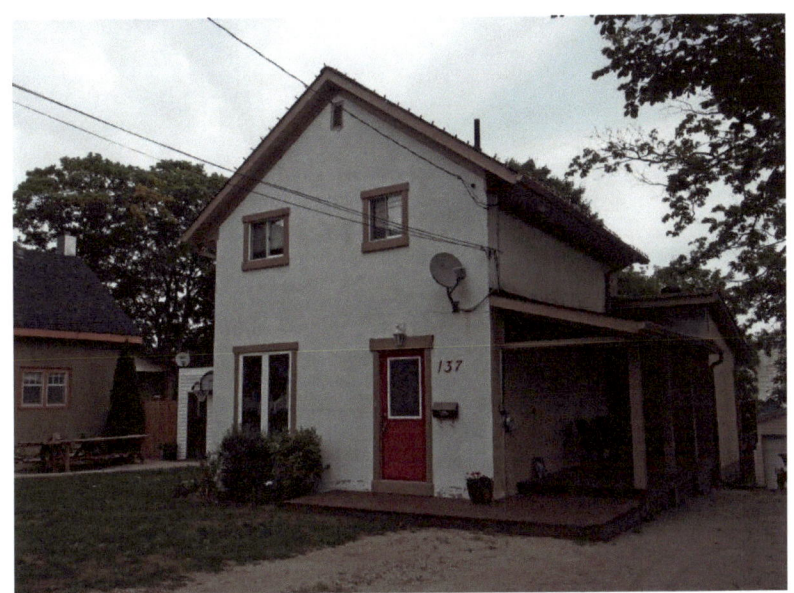

137 Fifth Street - Gothic

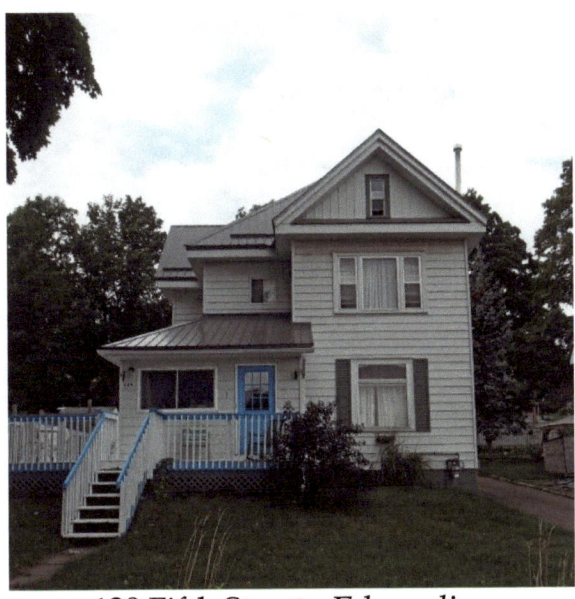

120 Fifth Street - Edwardian

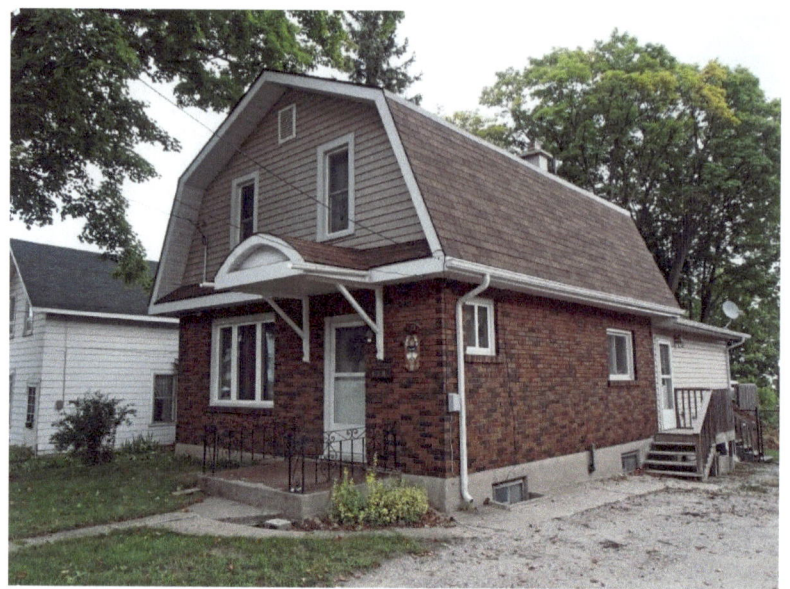

129 Fifth Street – Neo-colonial – gambrel roof

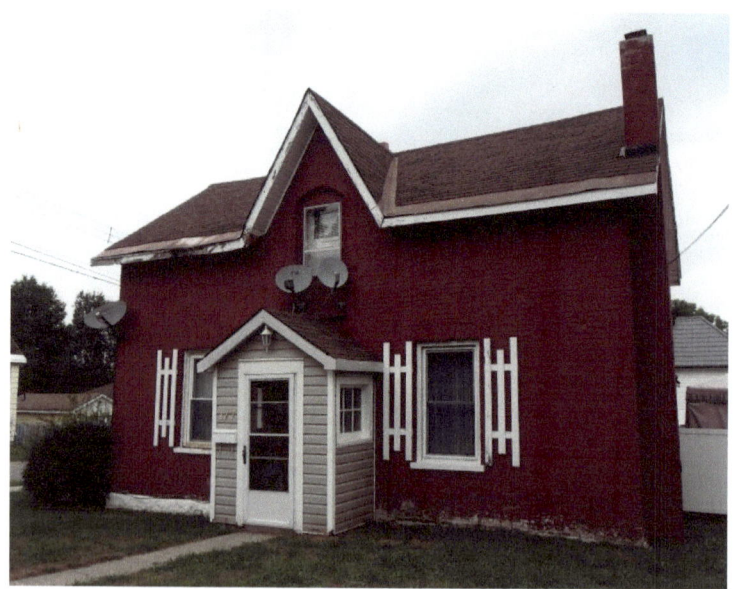

117 Fifth Street - Gothic

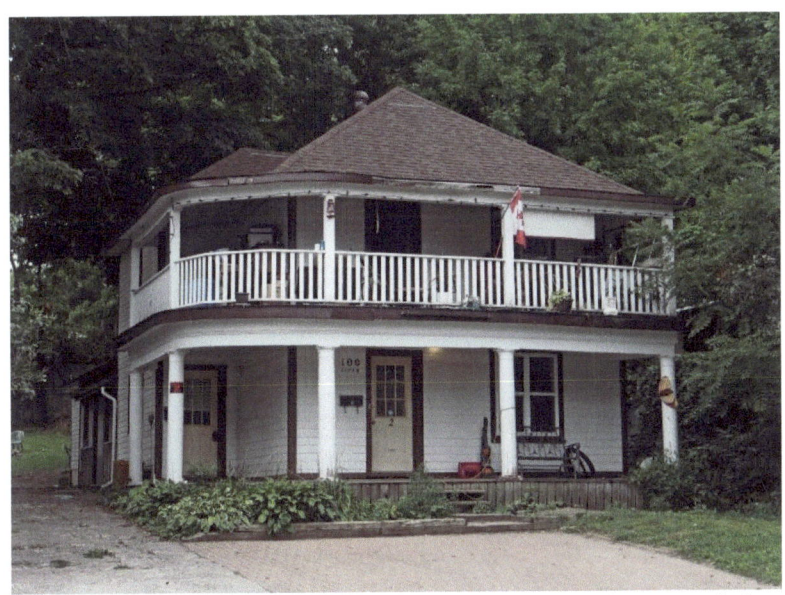

100 Fifth Street – two-storey wraparound verandah

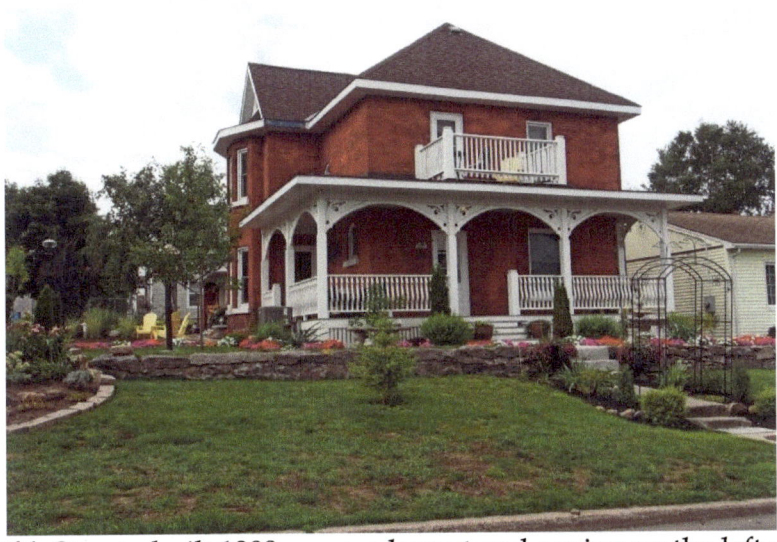

70 Fifth Street - built 1900, square layout and a wing on the left side; exterior is stretcher brick; upper storey balcony; medium hipped roof has an offset gable end on the façade and a molded frieze; semi-elliptical window on the left; open wooden veranda with decorative railings and support posts

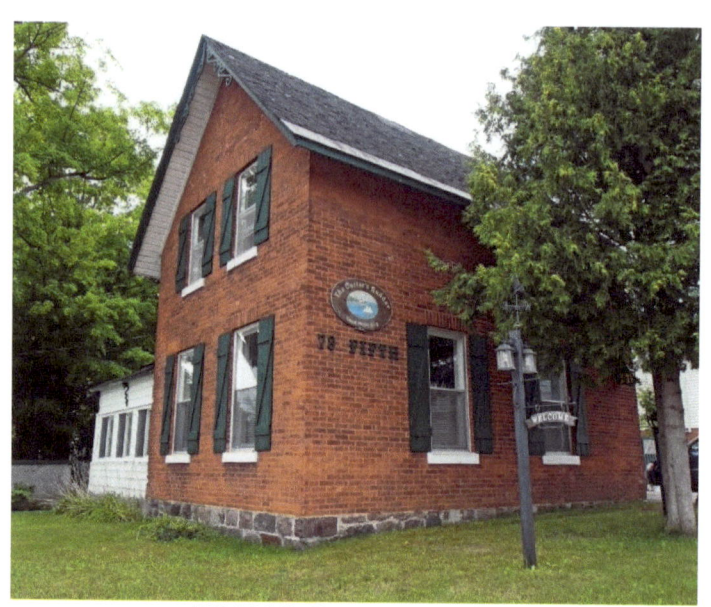

78 Fifth Street - Gothic

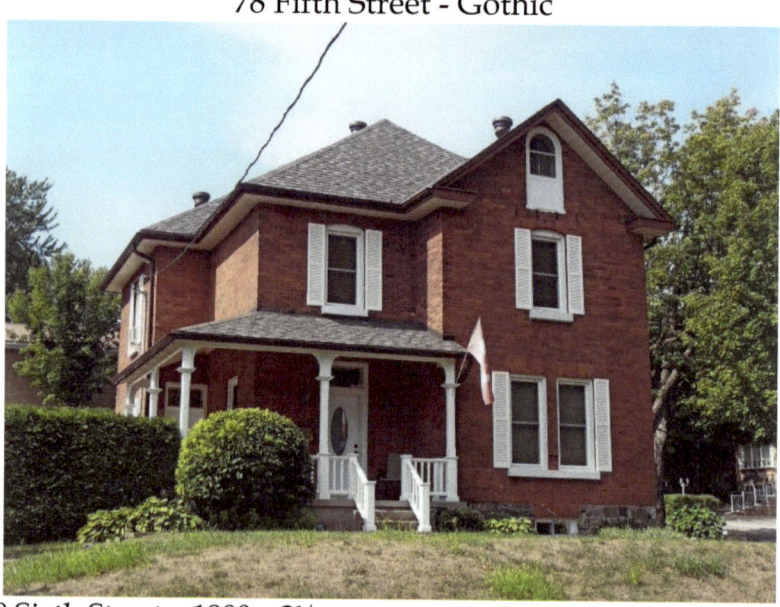

248 Sixth Street – 1900 – 2½ storeys; exterior is stretcher brick and broken course cut stone; pyramidal roof with an offset gable roof; upper storey door in gable with no balcony; brick voussoirs; transom window; open veranda with open railings, and decorative piers with Doric capitals

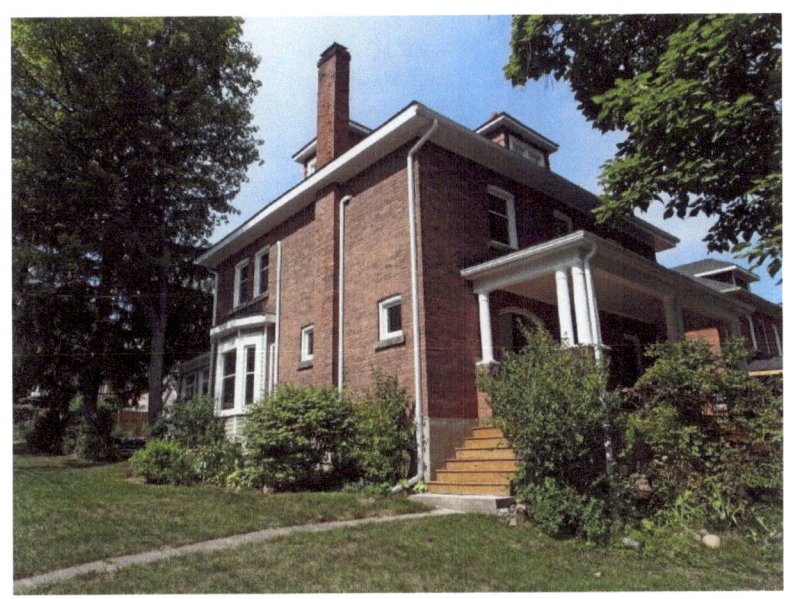

238 Sixth Street - dormers

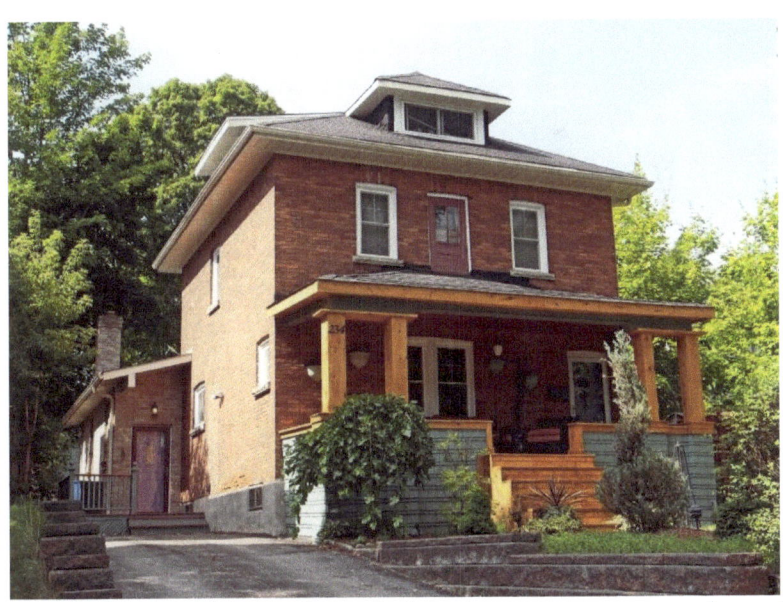

234 Sixth Street – hipped roof, dormers, square wooden piers for veranda

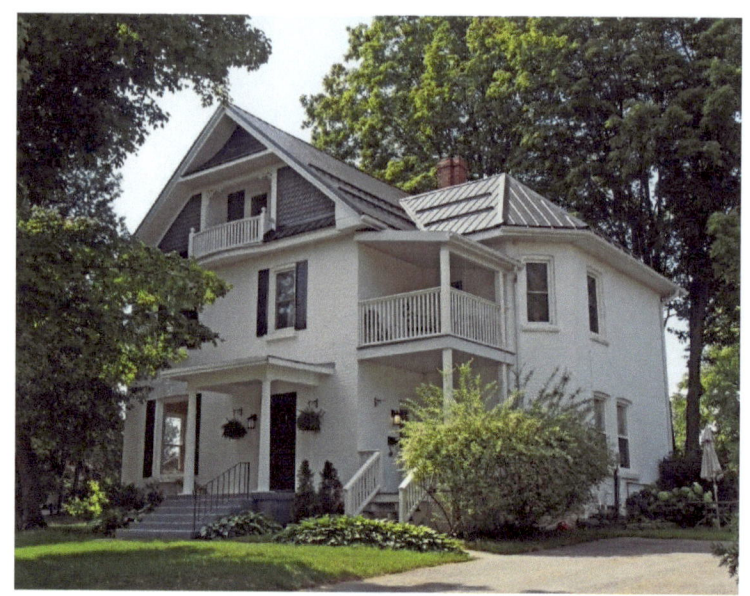

268 Sixth Street

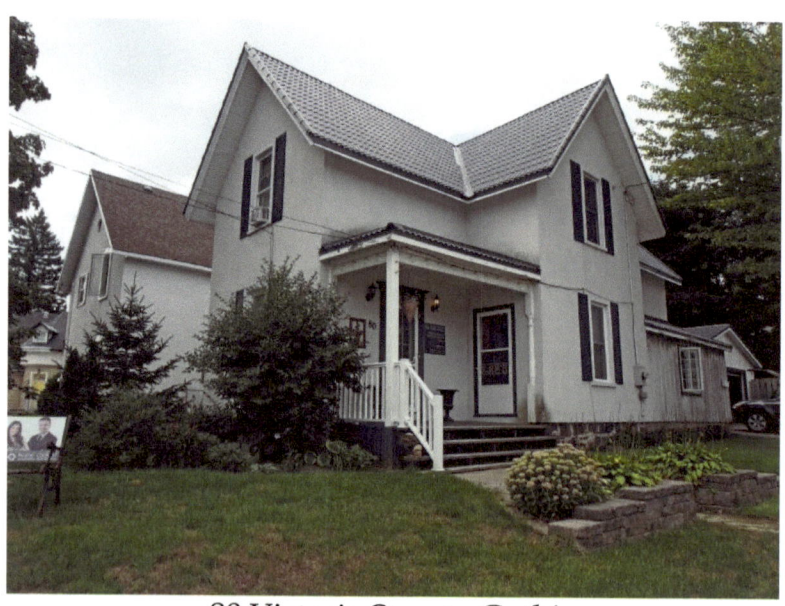

80 Victoria Street - Gothic

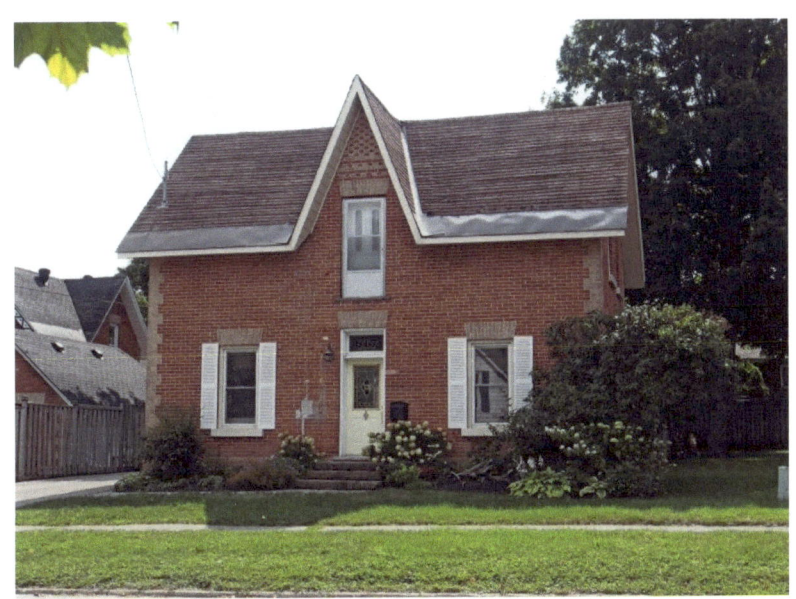

647 Dominion Avenue - Gothic

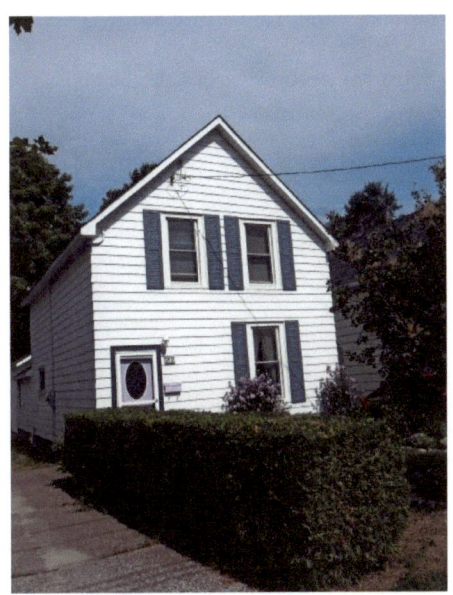

616 Dominion Avenue

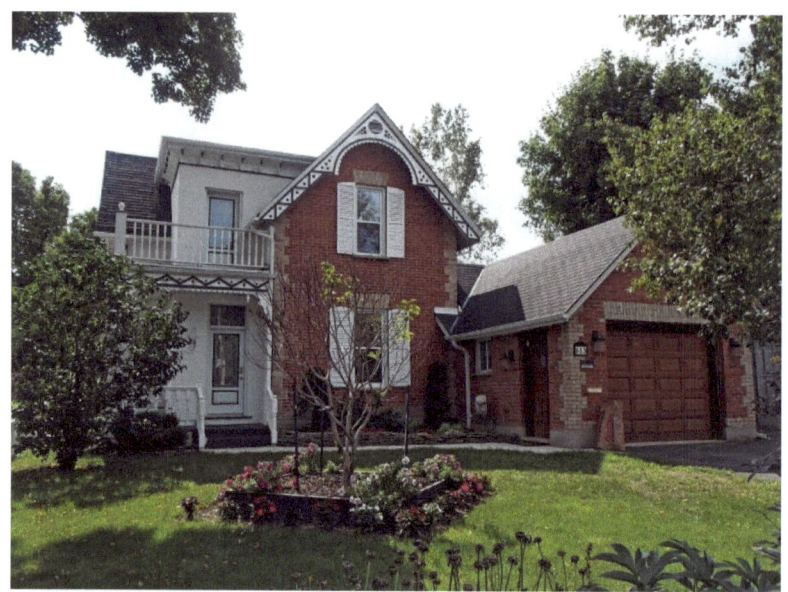

613 Dominion Avenue - built in 1900 – Vernacular - irregular layout and several different types of roofs, including flat, medium gable, and medium hipped, a decorated fascia; exterior is stretcher brick and poured concrete; upper storey balcony; windows with brick voussoirs; transom window; open platform veranda with decorated open railing and decorative trim along the roof line; wood piers to support the roof

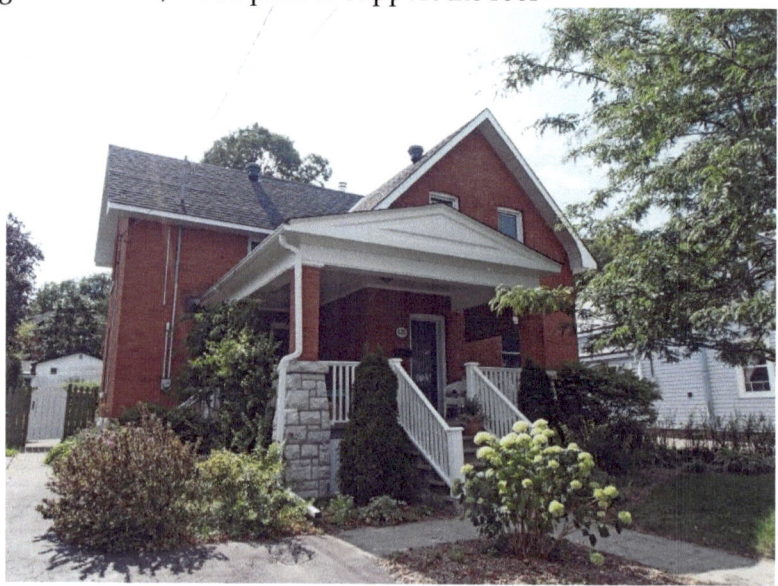

635 Dominion Avenue

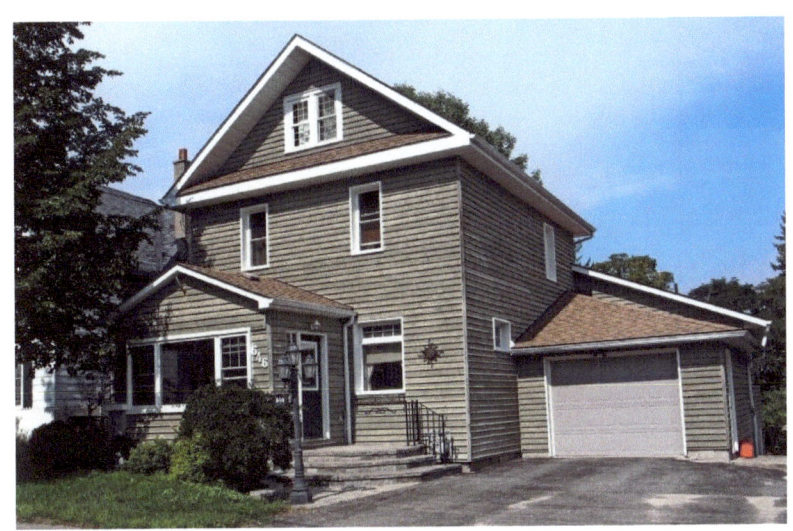

646 Dominion Avenue - Edwardian

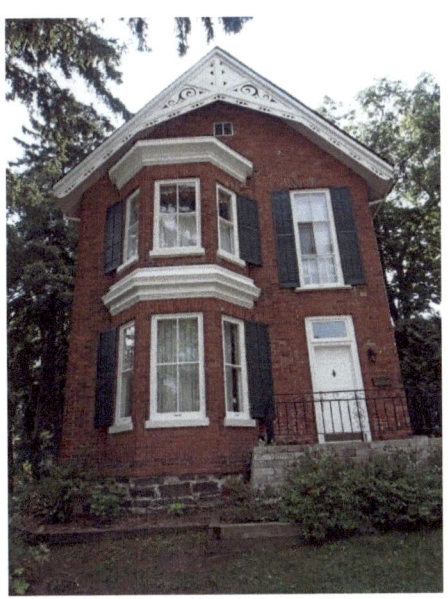

679 Dominion Avenue – two-storey bay window, verge board trim on gable

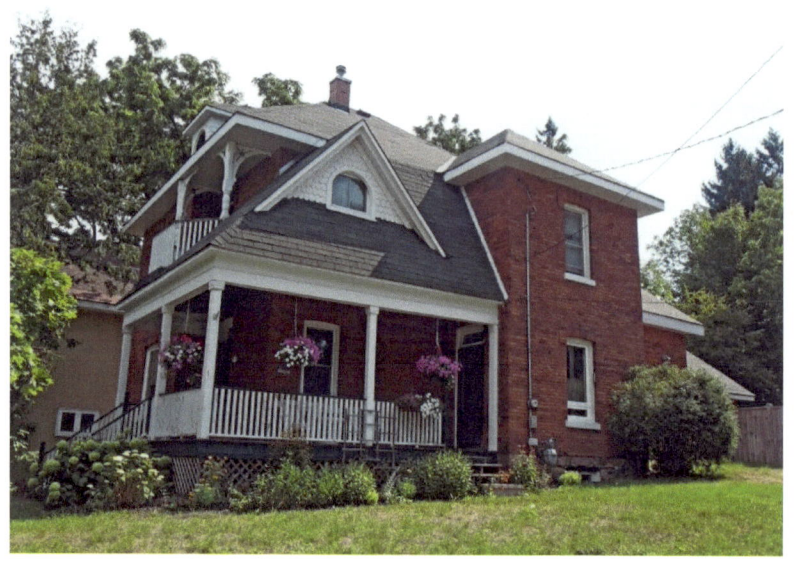

659 Dominion Avenue - built in 1892, a short rectangular
façade with wing on right; 2½ storey home; medium hipped
roof with a cross gable, a mansard dormer and a projecting
eaves gabled dormer; exterior has wood shingles, stretcher
brick, and even cut coarse stone; balcony with decorative
columns; brick voussoirs; dormers have semi-elliptical
windows; open veranda with open railings and piers for
support

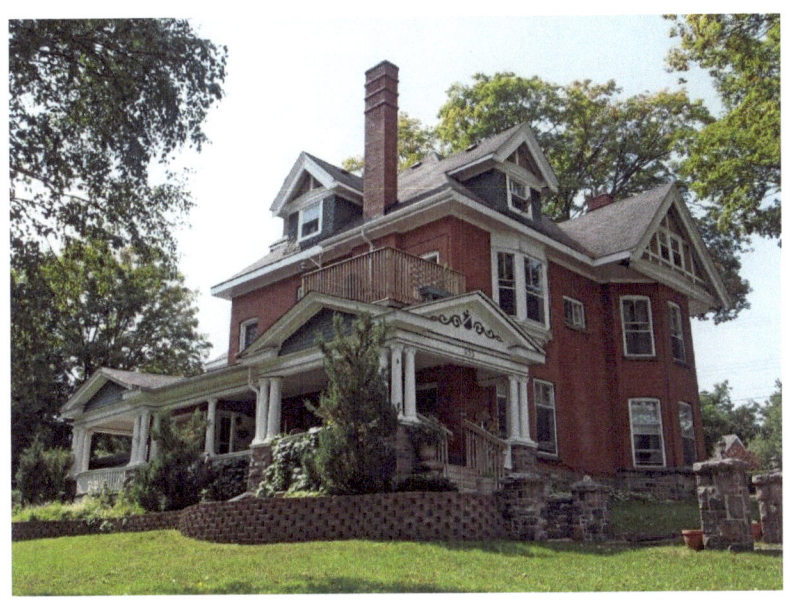

695 Dominion Avenue - built 1890, exterior of panel wood, broken course cut stone, stretcher brick, and terra cotta; medium gable roof, with decorated fascia and several gable ends with half timbering and gabled dormers; brick voussoirs; bay window on second storey; open veranda with open railing, stone, support pedestals, and Ionic capitals

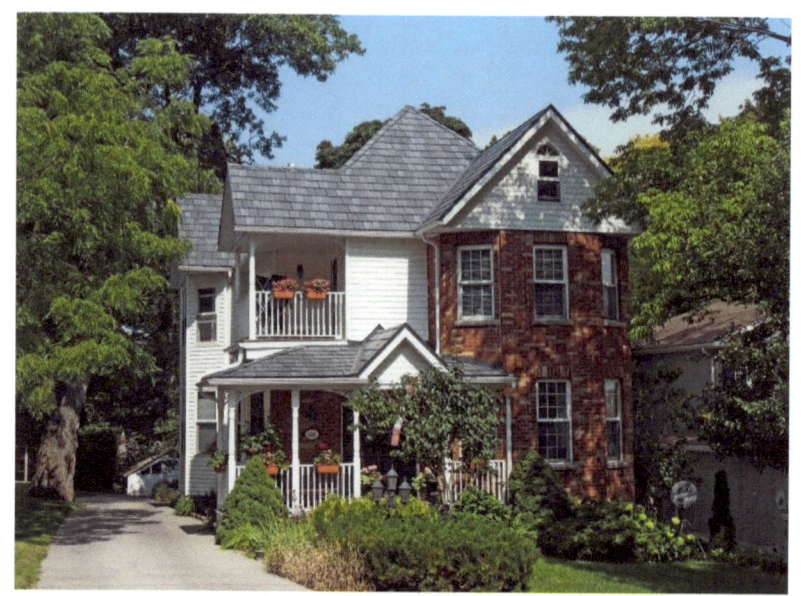

686 Dominion Avenue

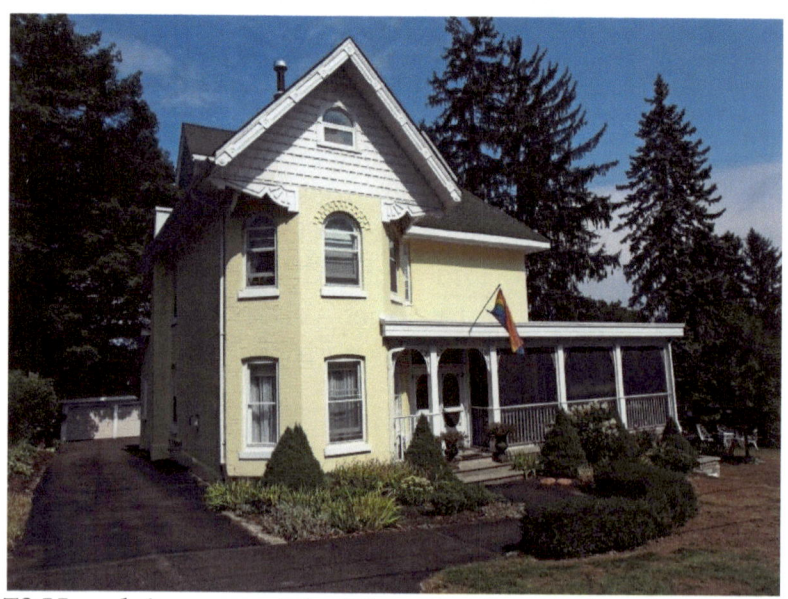

670 Hugel Avenue – The Victorian Inn Bed and Breakfast

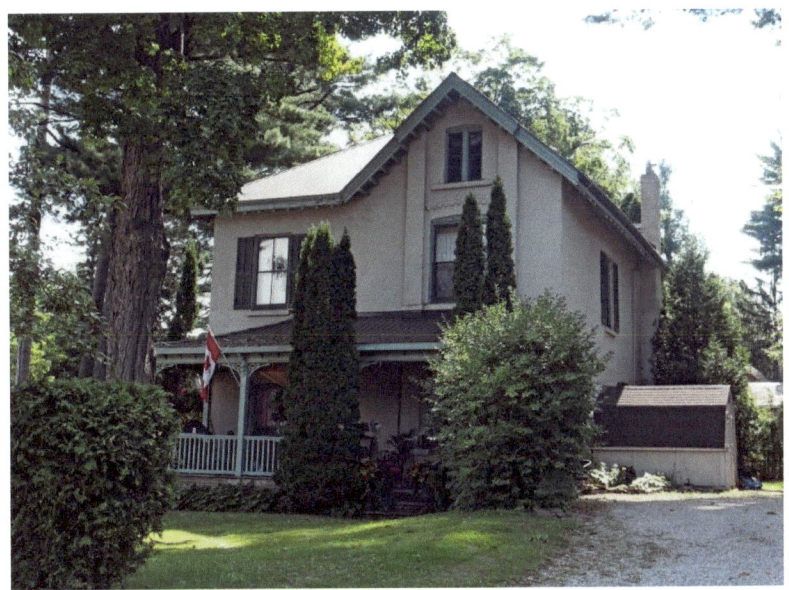

Hugel Avenue

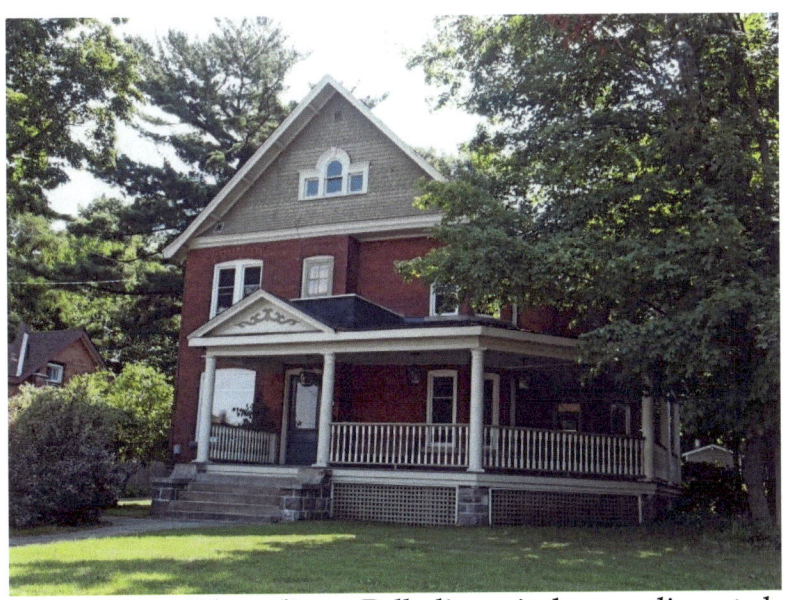

Hugel Avenue – Edwardian – Palladian window, pediment above
pillared veranda with open railing

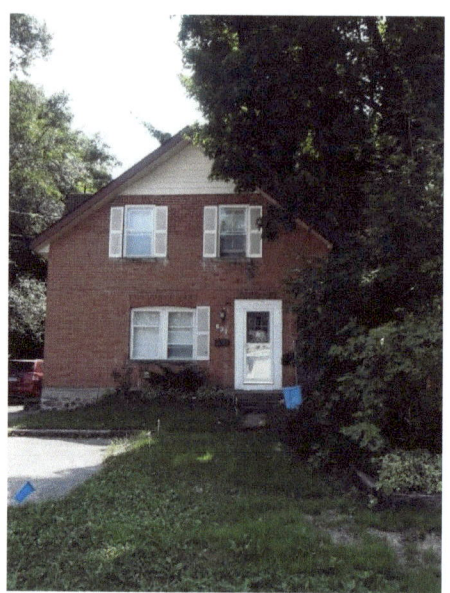

637 Hugel Avenue

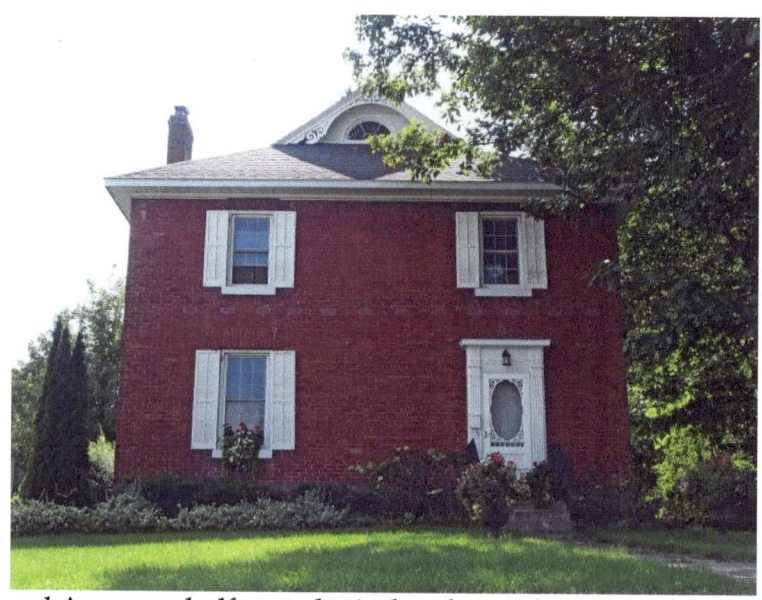

Hugel Avenue - half round window located in the upper storey dormer

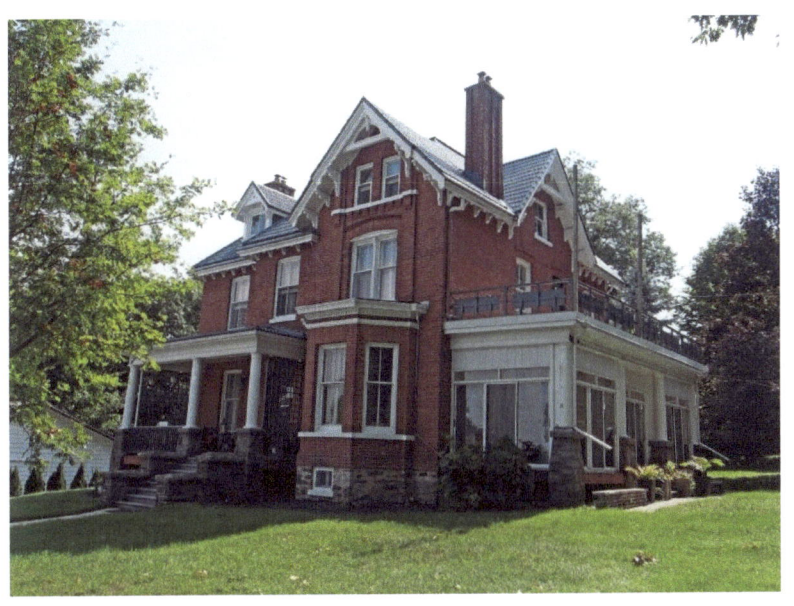

657 Hugel Avenue - The Dollar House is the former residence of two of Midland's leading historical figures: John Dollar (Ontario Lumber Company) and William Finlayson (lawyer, cabinet minister). Decorative gable ends, bracket roof trim, bay windows; medium hipped roof with several gables and gable roofed dormers; window voussoirs; two chimneys

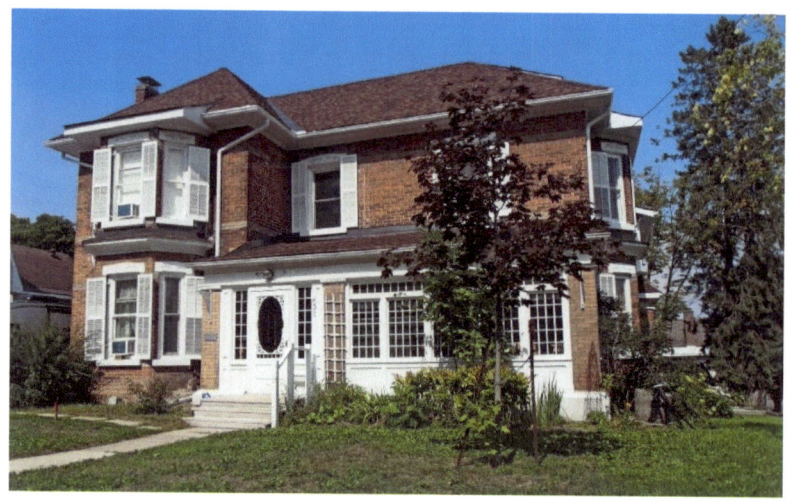

632 Hugel Avenue - built in 1920 - 2½ storey, brick and clapboard exterior; truncated pyramidal roof with a shed dormer; string course wraps around the house; closed in upper storey balcony; bay windows; sidelights; open porch has stone supports with brick piers and is constructed of concrete and brick; closed porch has brick piers, several windows and is constructed of wood and brick; decorative trim around the roof and the top of the wall

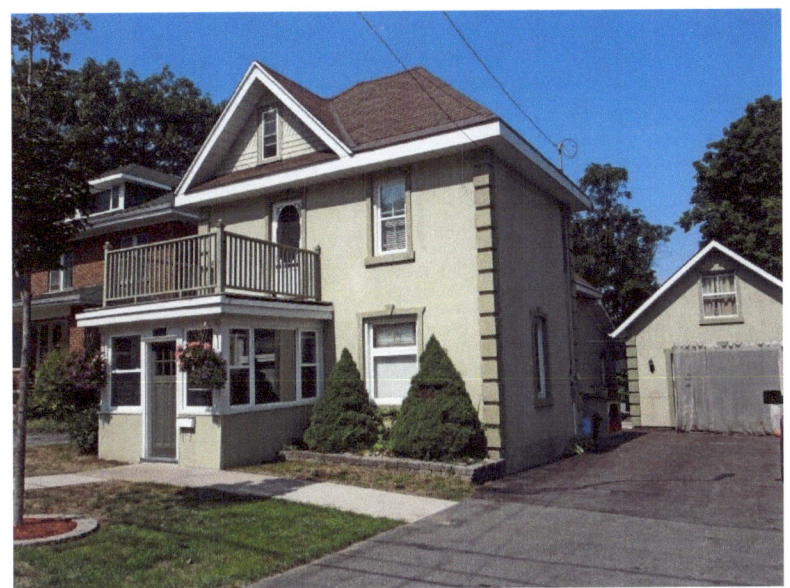

Hugel Avenue – dormers, corner quoins, second floor balcony with open railing with closed porch below

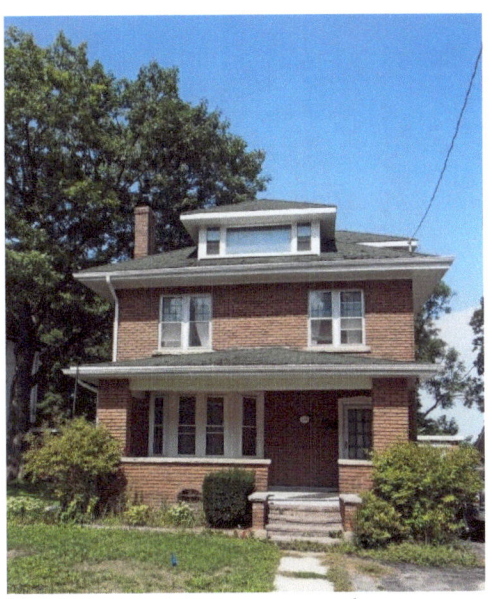

640 Hugel Avenue - dormer

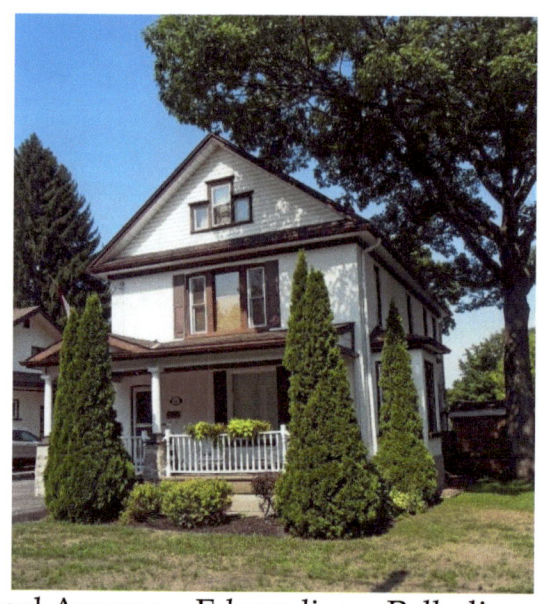

644 Hugel Avenue – Edwardian – Palladian window

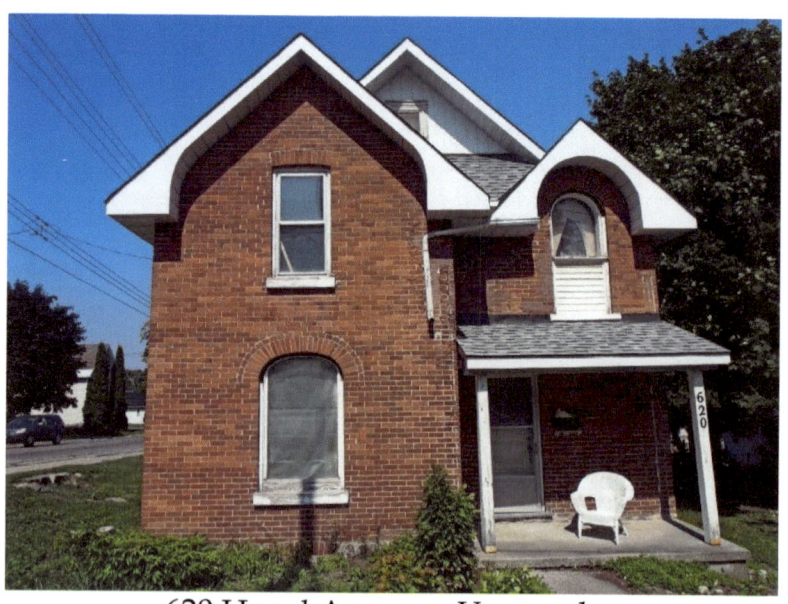

620 Hugel Avenue - Vernacular

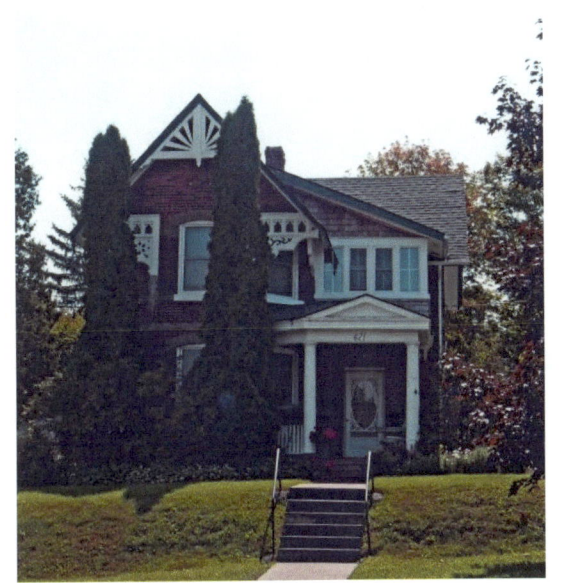

621 Hugel Avenue – Gothic – trim on gable

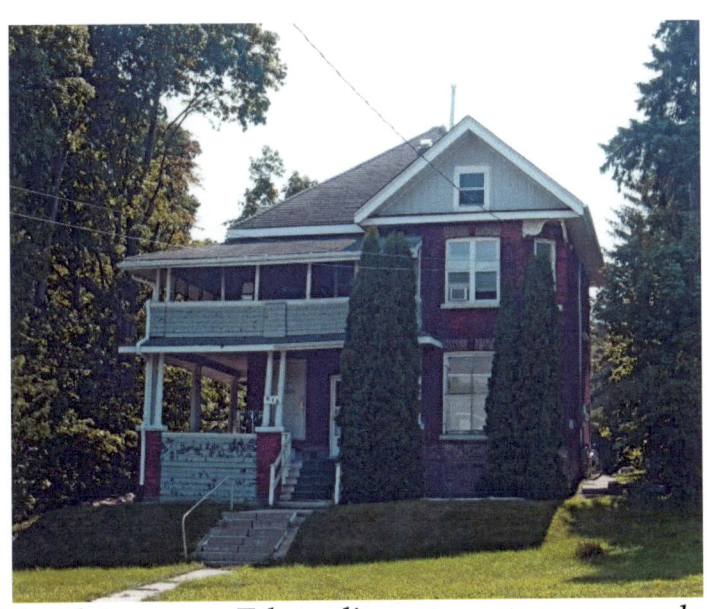

615 Hugel Avenue – Edwardian – two storey veranda with closed railings

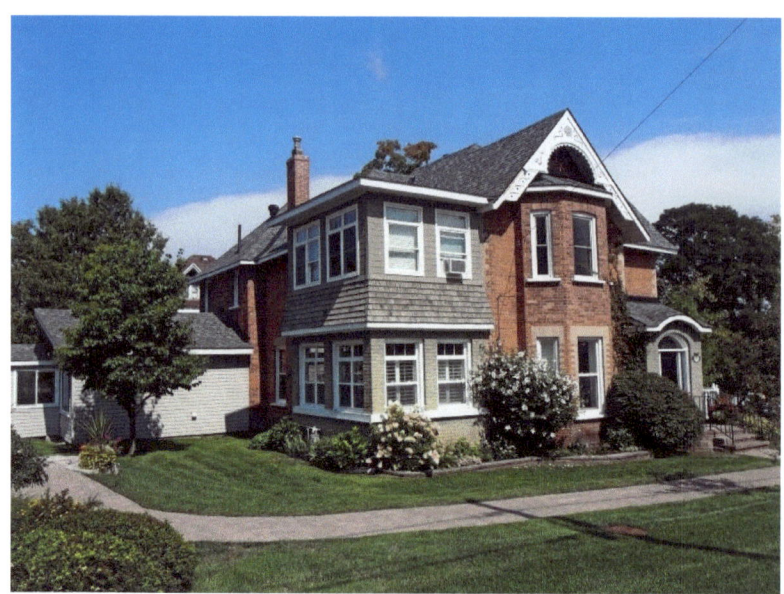

600 Hugel Avenue – Victorian – built between 1870 and 1890 -
ornate gingerbread

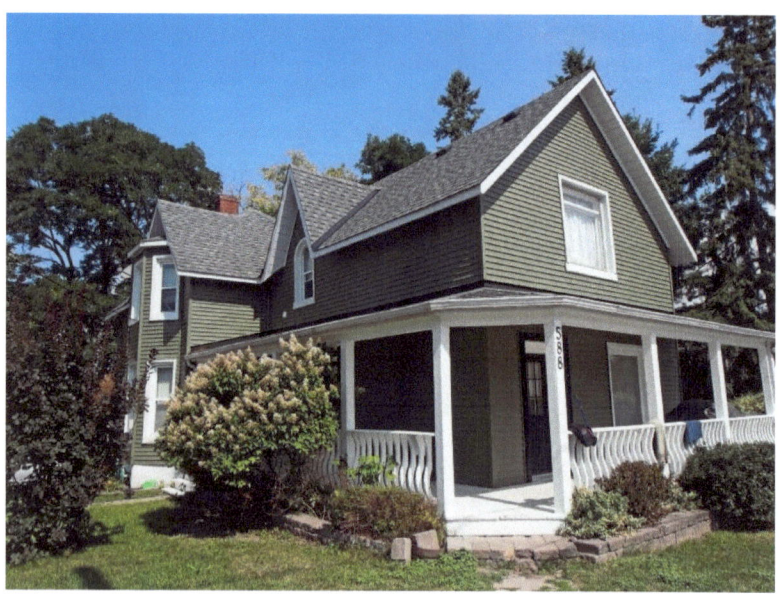

588 Hugel Avenue - Gothic

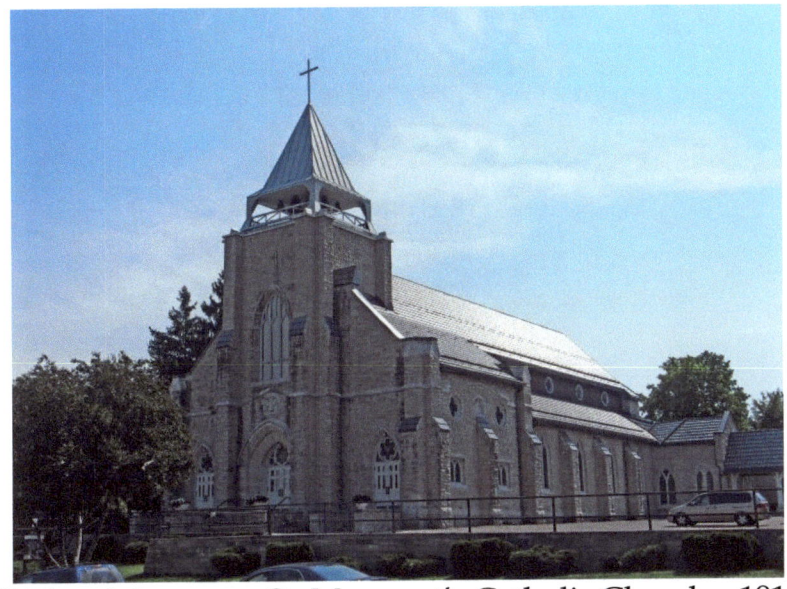

589 Hugel Avenue – St. Margaret's Catholic Church – 1914 – Gothic - rose windows, buttresses, quatrefoils, muntins in large window above main portal, eight bells donated for the tower

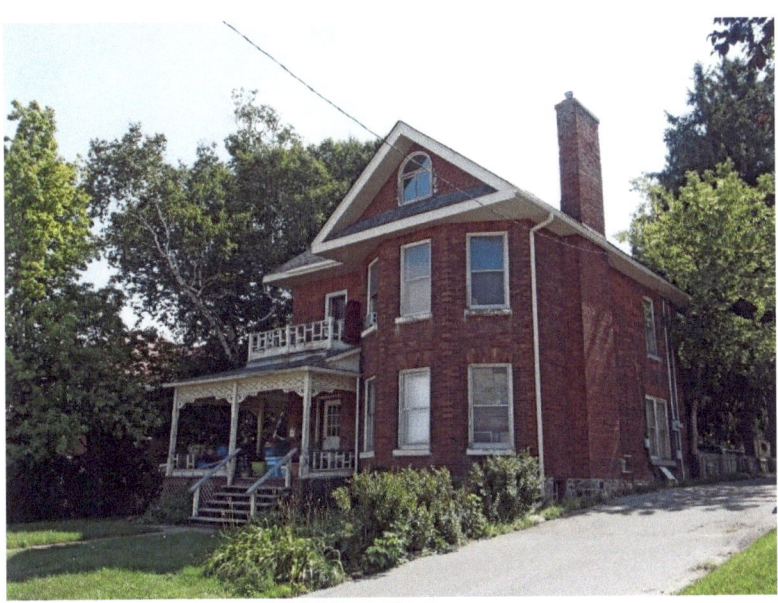

677 Hugel Avenue

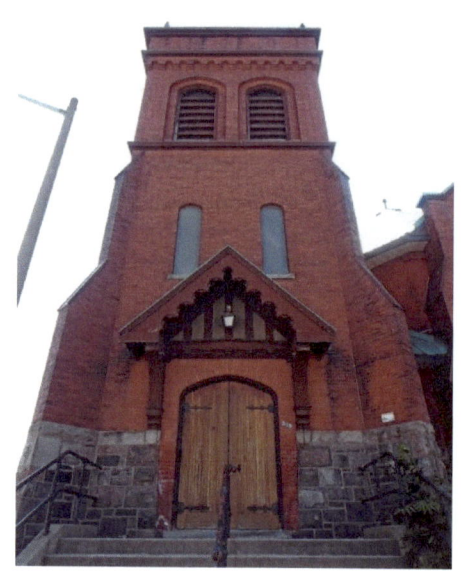

539 Hugel Avenue - Knox A Different Kind of Church – 1902
Romanesque style

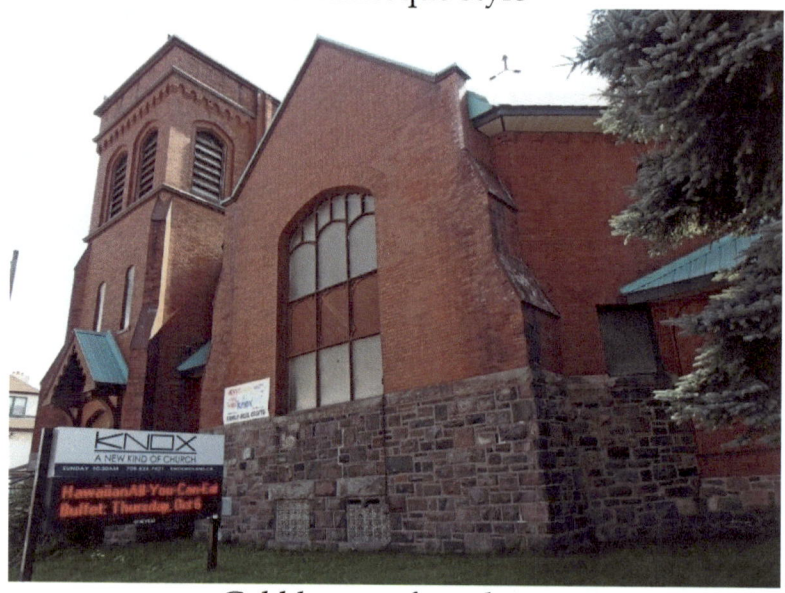

Cobblestone foundation

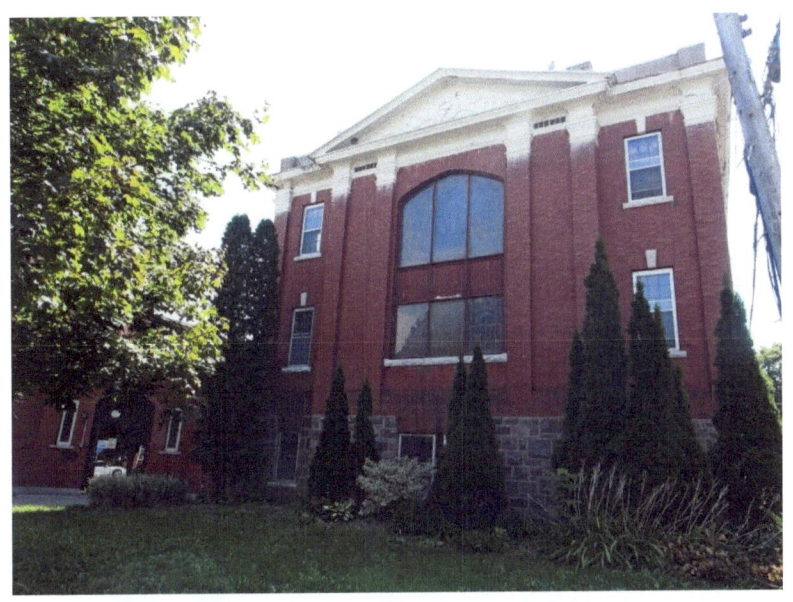

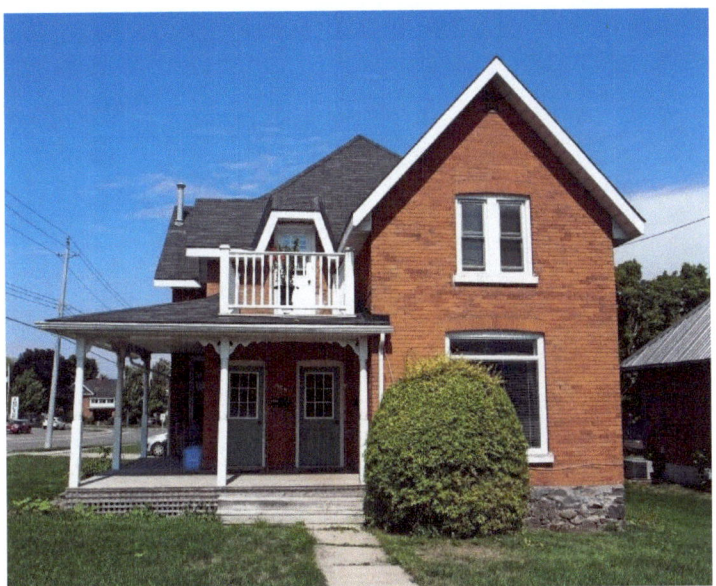

558 Hugel Avenue

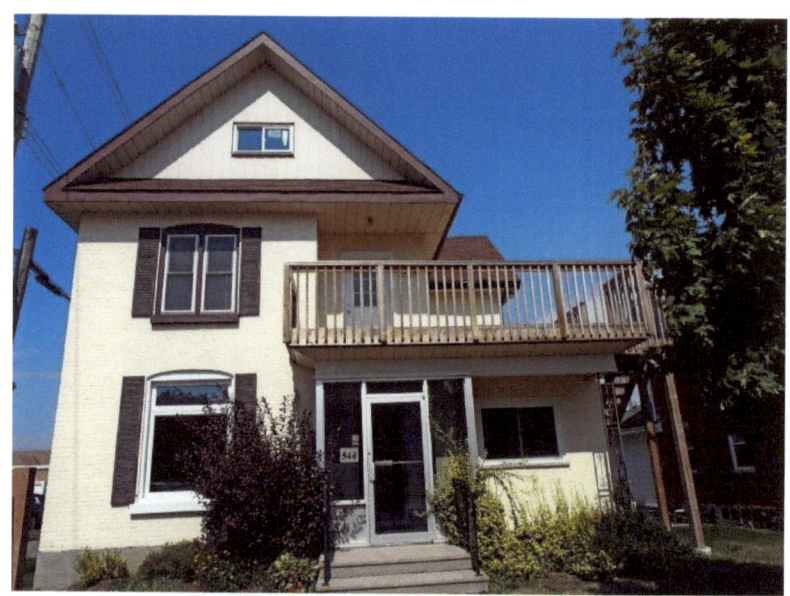

544 Hugel Avenue - Edwardian

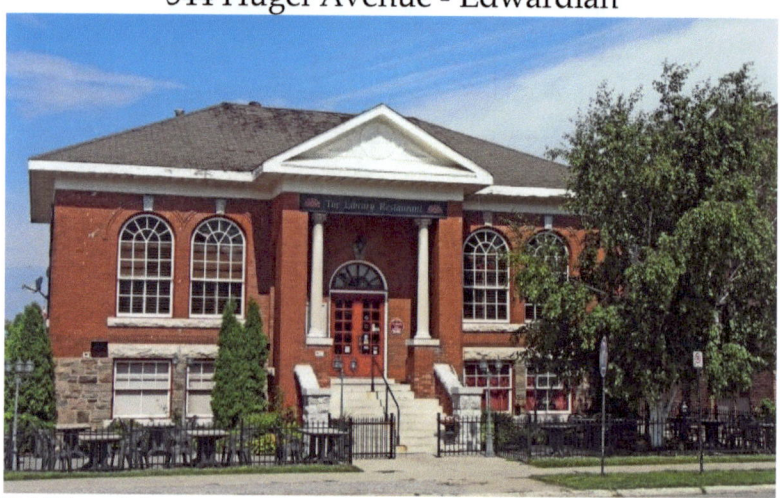

526 Hugel Avenue - The Library Restaurant is in the original
Carnegie Library, built in 1915 – Edwardian Classical - stretcher
brick façade, pilasters and piers enhance the frontispiece; medium
hip, truncated roof; semi-circular windows with brick keystones;
multi-light shaped transom above the two leaf door; open main
porch constructed of brick and cement with closed railings

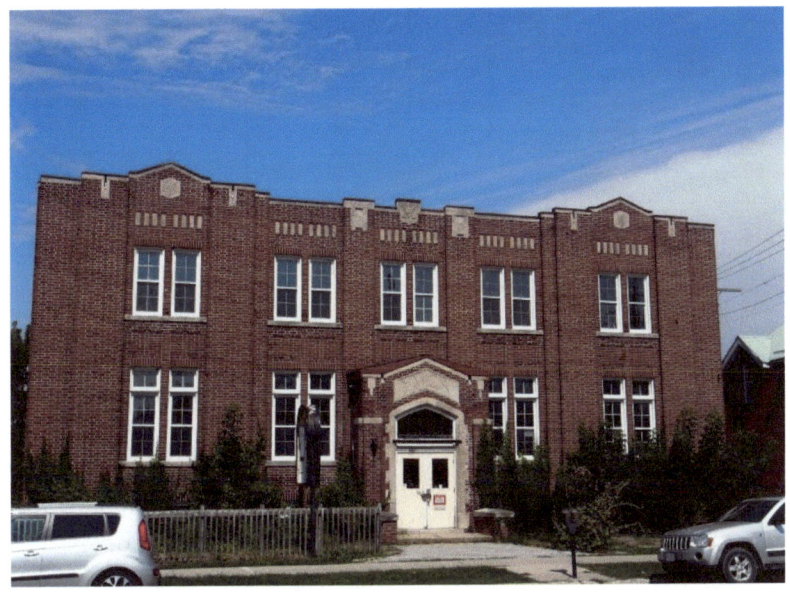

Hugel Avenue - the Midland chapter of the Young Men's Christian Association founded in 1900 - building built in 1929 with a gymnasium, reading room, rooms for members, and a parlour for use by members. In 1980 building was bought by Budd Watson, an internationally known local photographer who opened a gallery to display his signature photographs.

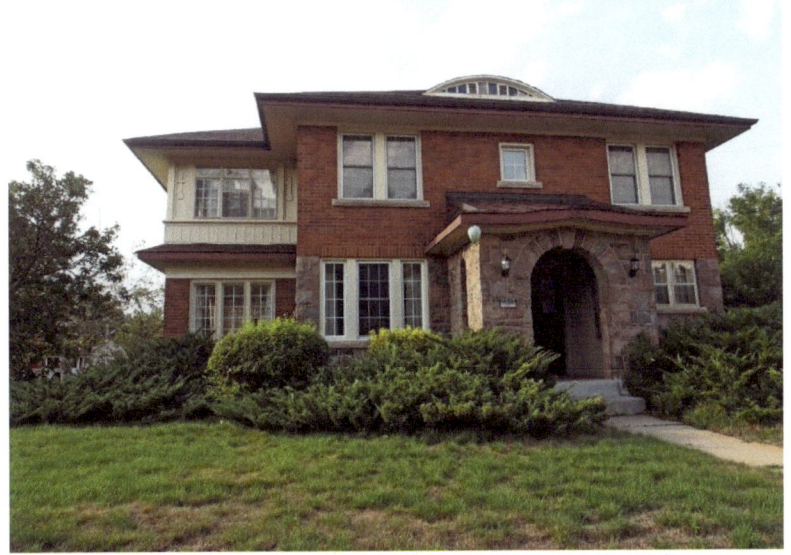

356 Hugel Avenue – Midland Heritage building

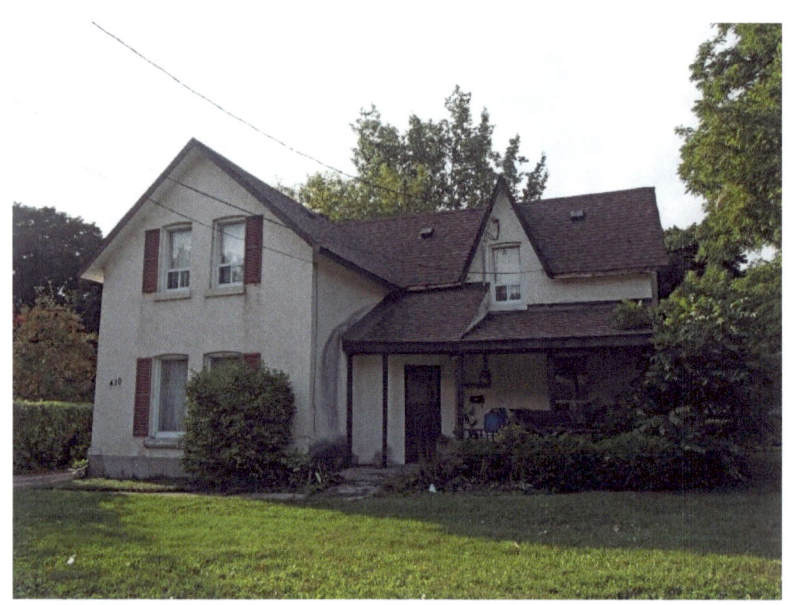

410 Hugel Avenue

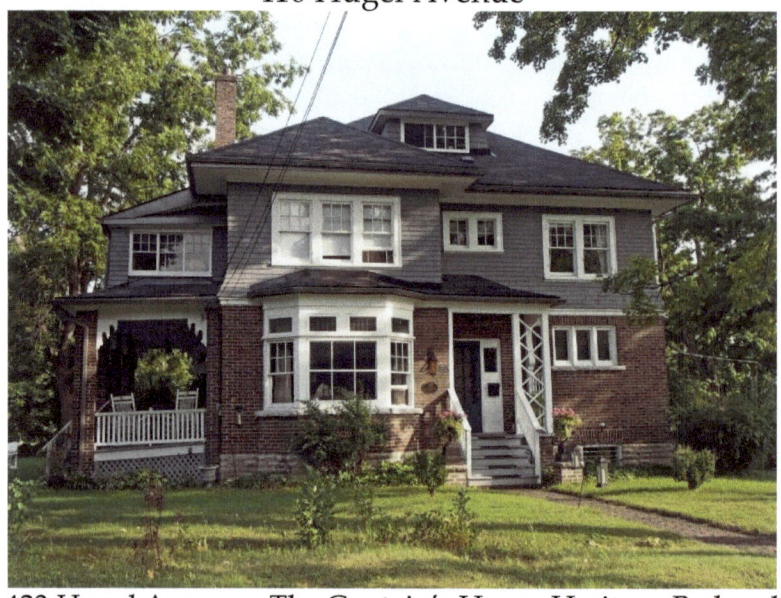

423 Hugel Avenue - The Captain's House Heritage Bed and
Breakfast - built 1900 - Edwardian Classicism style, low gabled roof,
siding and brick façade, numerous windows and a stone
foundation; large bay window

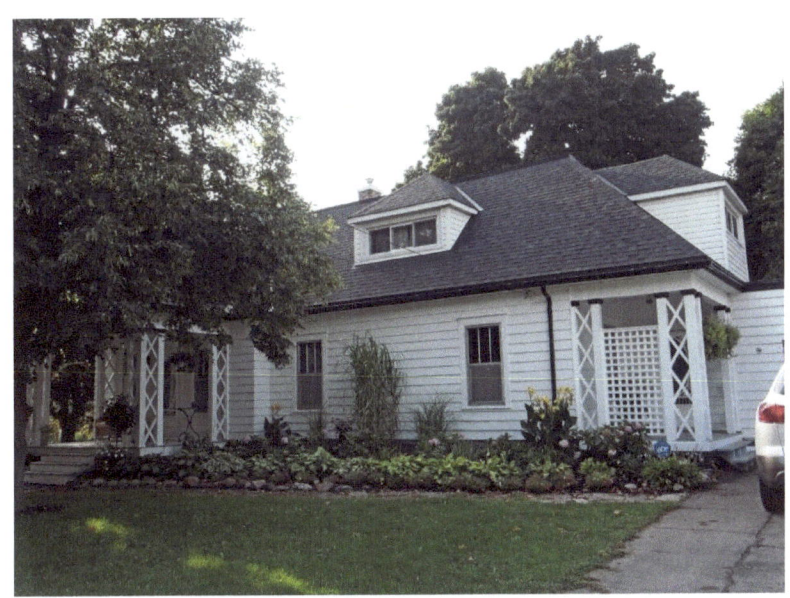

Hugel Avenue

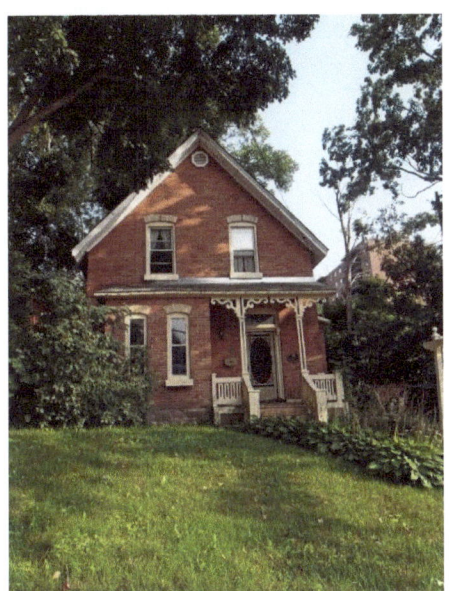

441 Hugel Avenue – c. 1895 - Gothic

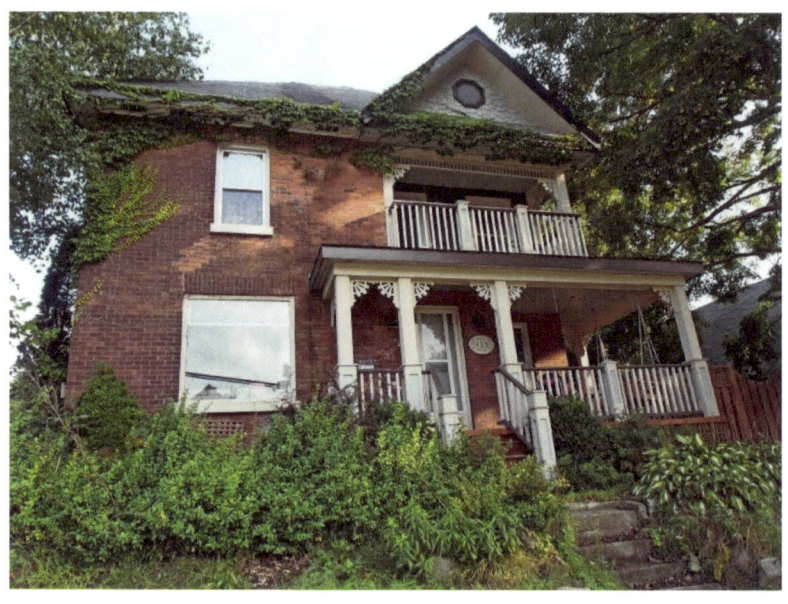

435 Hugel Avenue - Built in 1903 – 2½ storey Queen Anne style, large gable end on the front; several verandas and porches under the gables and eaves; full below ground basement; mainly brick exterior with wood shingling in the upper gable end; poured concrete foundation; high hip roof with a truncated center; octagonal window in gable; open veranda with decorative railings

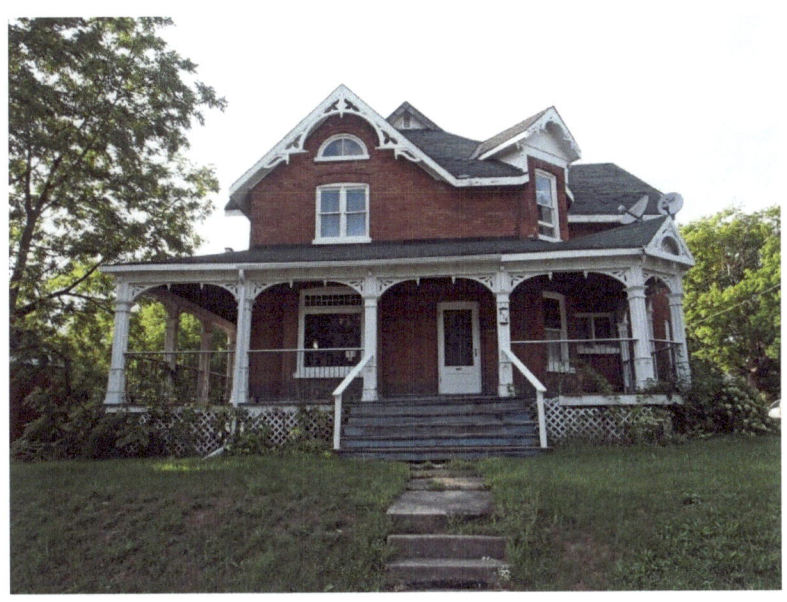

434 Hugel Avenue - built 1897 by William Hope, once owned by John Bruce Hanly, husband of Eliza Adele Burke, sister of the Burke Captains. Decorative gable ends, gingerbread trim on front porch, bay windows; medium hipped roof with offset gable, and gable roofed dormers; window voussoirs; half window on second storey

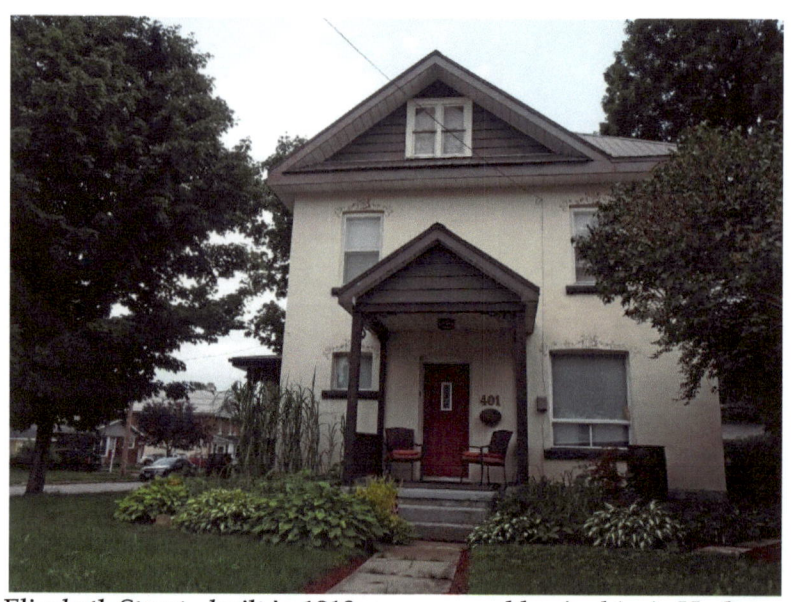

401 Elizabeth Street - built in 1910, once owned by Archie A. Hudson who sailed many ships for James Playfair. Edwardian style - white stucco façade with clap board at the top in the gable; hipped roof; decorative painted area above the windows

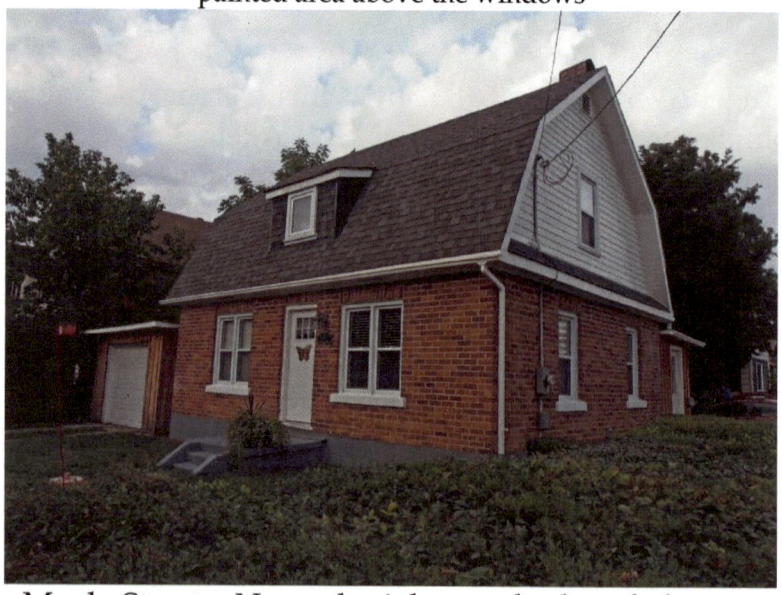

Manly Street – Neo-colonial – gambrel roof, dormer

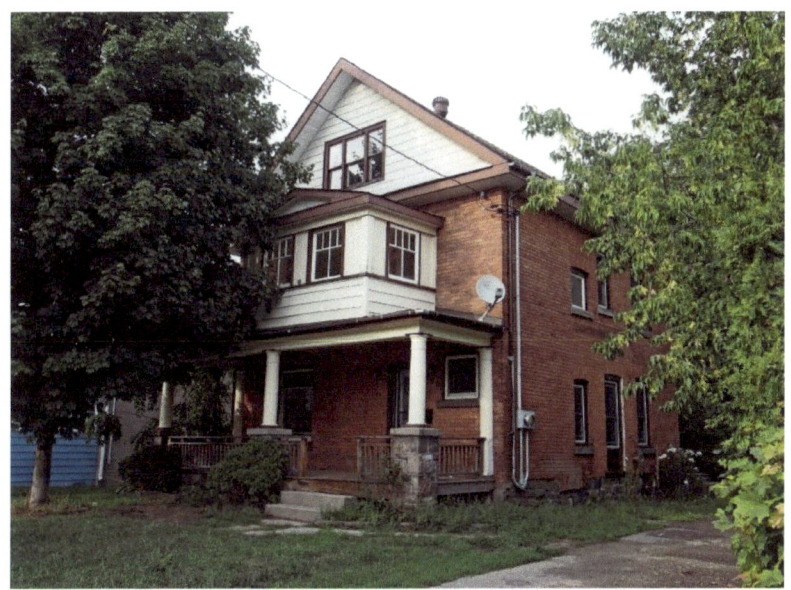

Manly Street - Edwardian

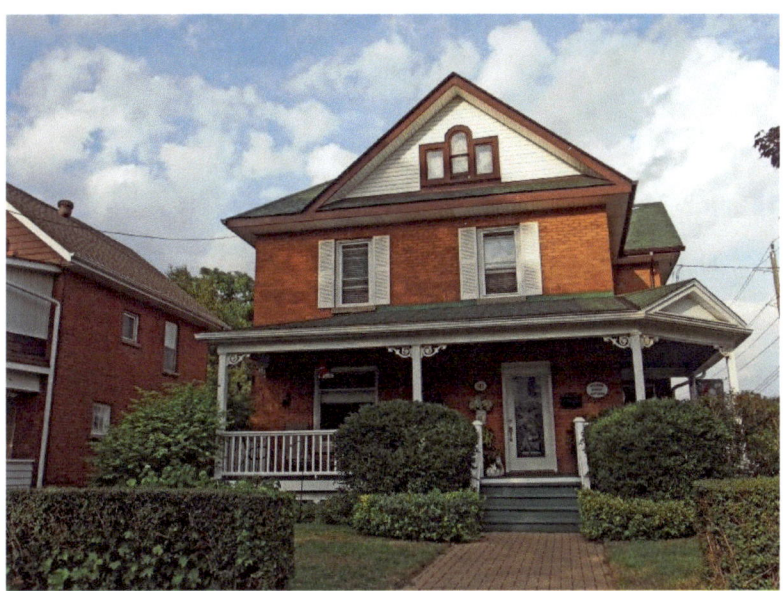

Manly Street - Edwardian – Palladian window in gable,
decorative veranda supports, open railing, pediment

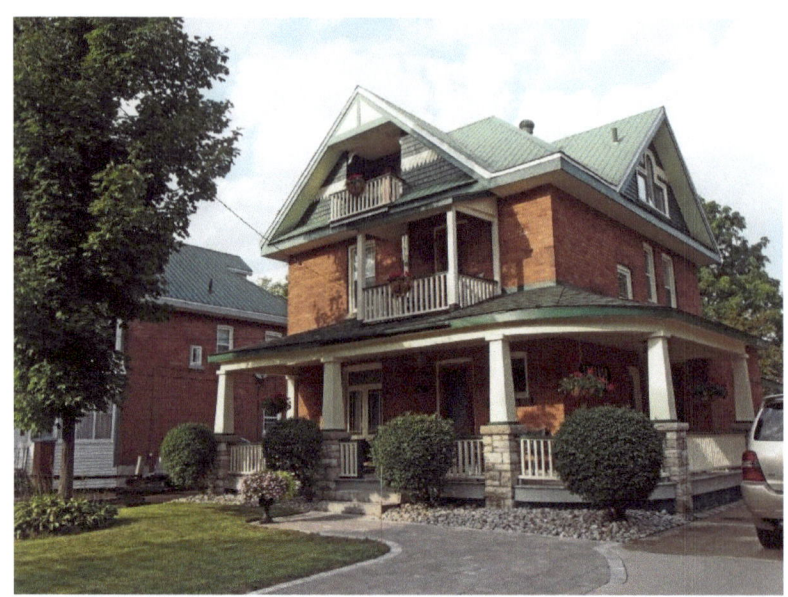

401 Manly Street – 2½ storeys; stretcher brick and wood shingle exterior; pyramidal roof with two cross gables; two balconies with open railings and decorative supports; brick voussoirs; Palladian windows in gables; wraparound veranda with stone supports, decorative piers, and open railings

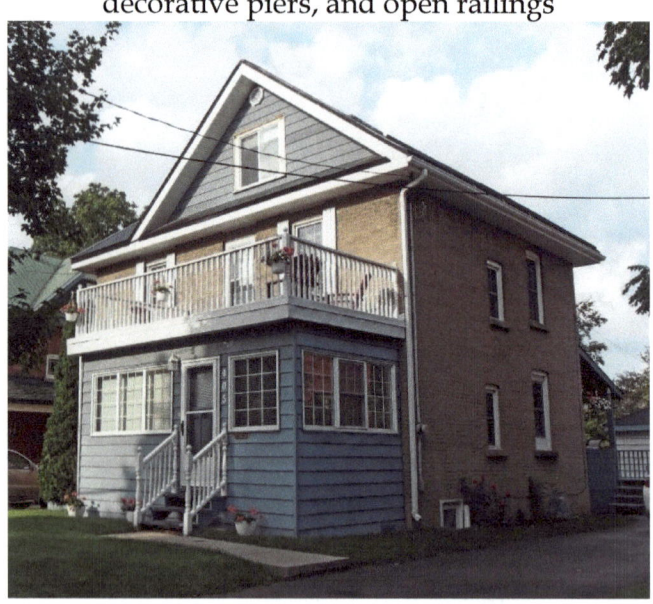

405 Manly Street - Edwardian

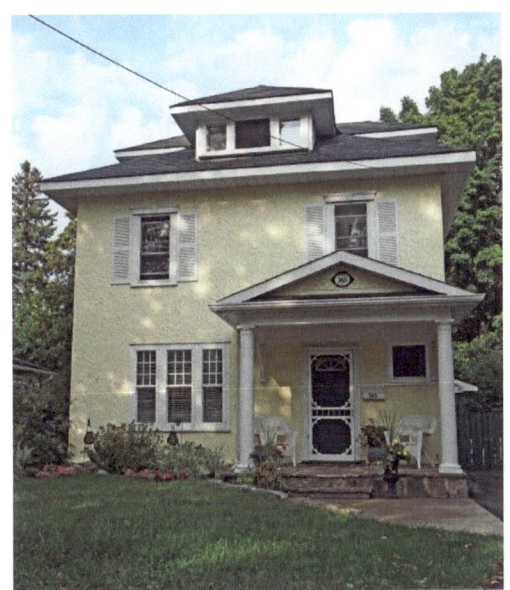

365 Manly Street – dormer, pediment

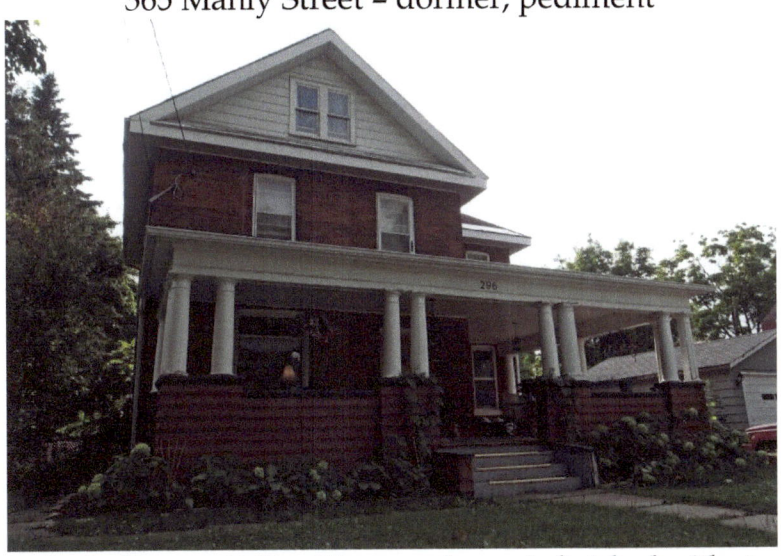

298 Manly Street – 1910 – 2½ storey home is finished with stone, brick, and clapboard; inset second storey balcony; medium hipped roof has a large dormer in the front; brick voussoirs; open veranda with wood shingle cover supports and Edwardian colonettes; upper storey balcony located on roof of veranda

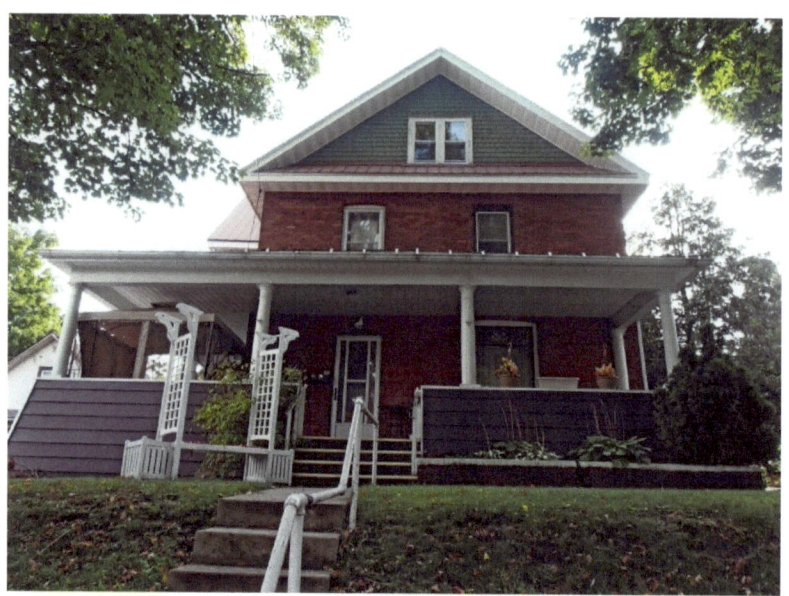

302 Manly Street – c. 1905-1910 - Edwardian Classicism – 2½ storey, red stretcher brick home with shingles in the upper dormer; medium hipped roof; veranda supported by seven gently tapered smooth columns with Doric capitals; brick voussoirs

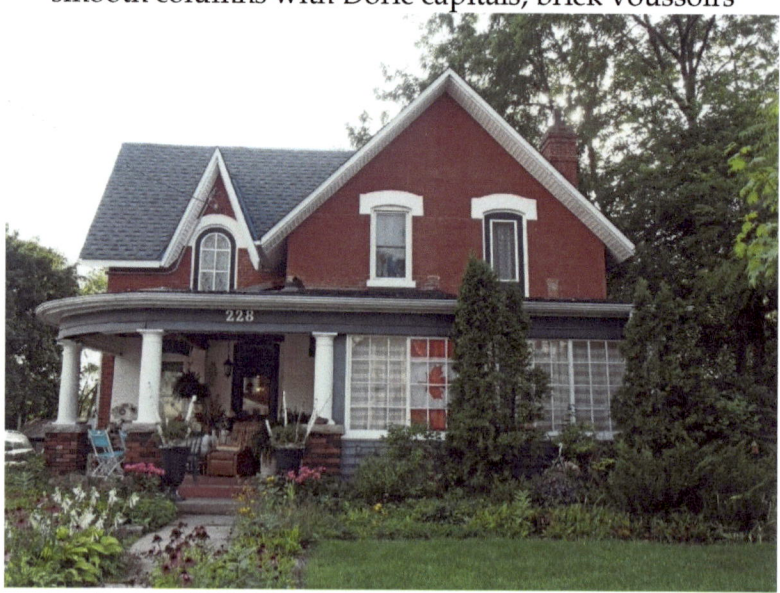

228 Manly Street - Victorian

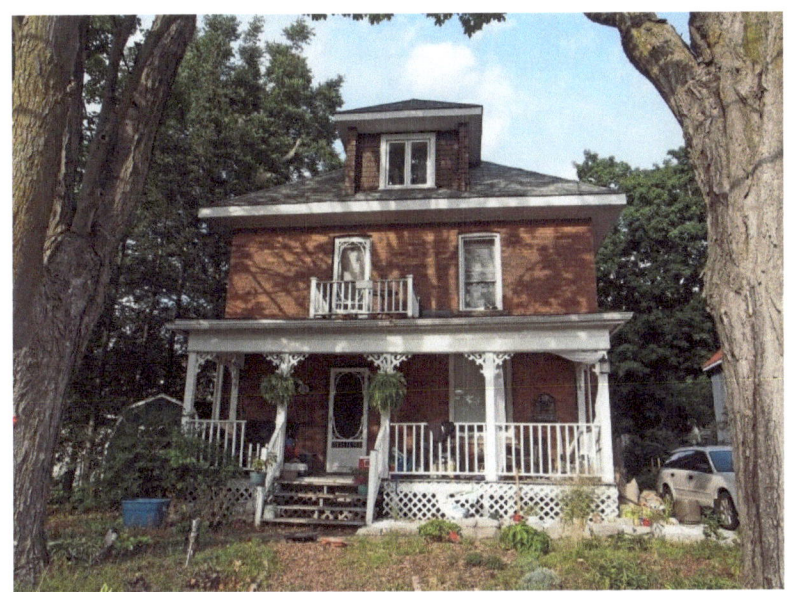

225 Manly Street – dormer, decorative posts on veranda, open railing, second floor balcony

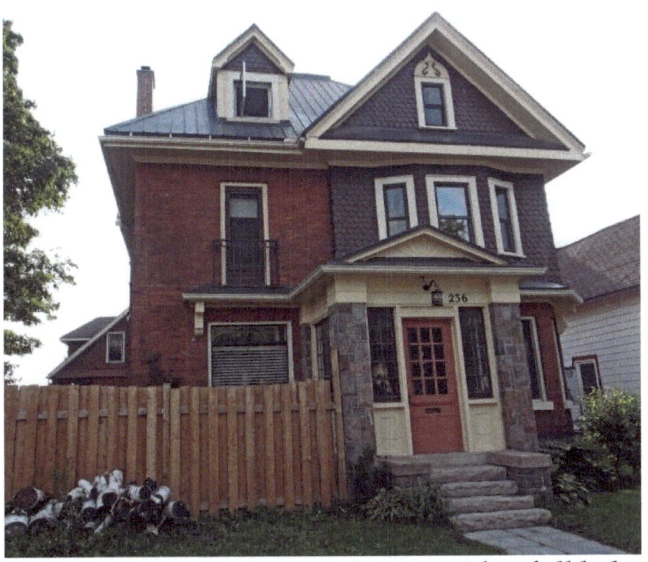

236 Manly Street – 1900 – 2½ storey house with a full below ground basement; exterior is stretcher brick with even cut stone on the closed porch and wood shingles on the upper storey offset gable; dormer; sidelights

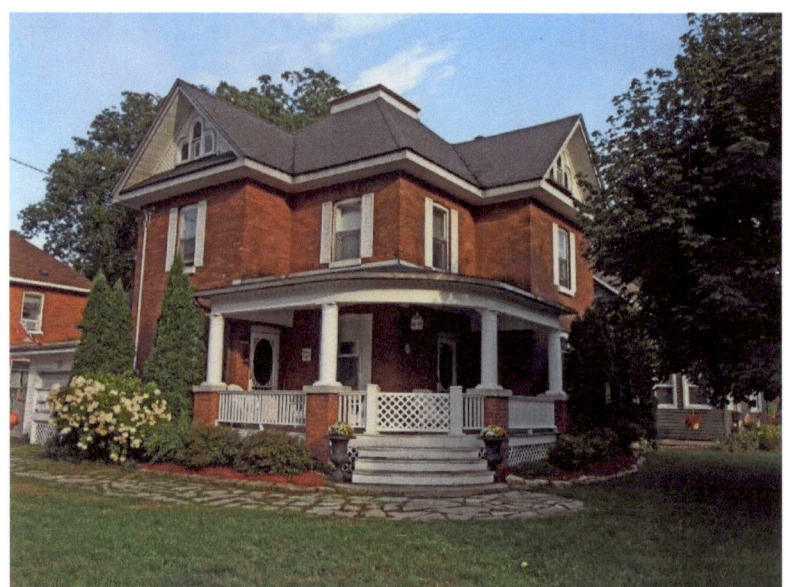

421 Midland Avenue - square floor plan with wings on all four sides; former manse of Baptist Church; exterior is stretcher brick and terra cotta; truncated pyramidal roof with a gable end on each side; windows with brick voussoirs, wooden shutters; Palladian windows in gables; wraparound veranda with opening railings, decorative roof trim, brick supports with Doric capital posts

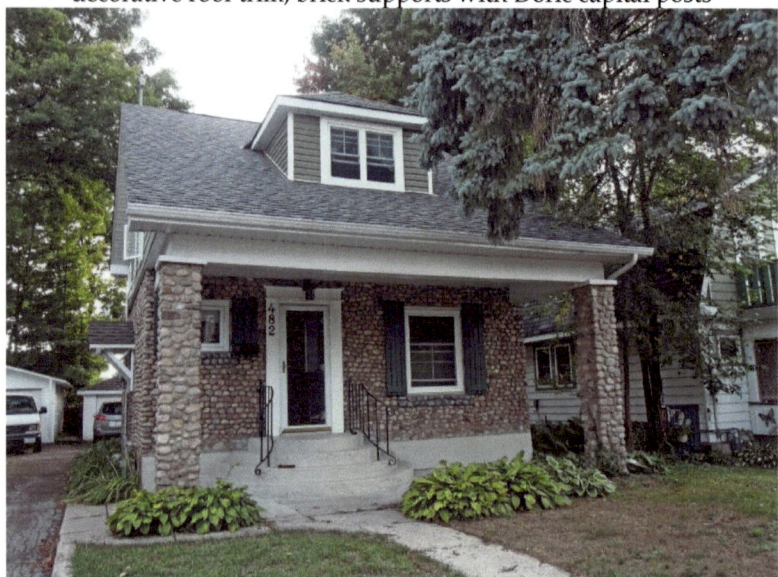

482 Midland Avenue – 1930 - exterior is clap board and plain field stone; medium gable roof has an overhang to cover the front entrance; hipped dormer

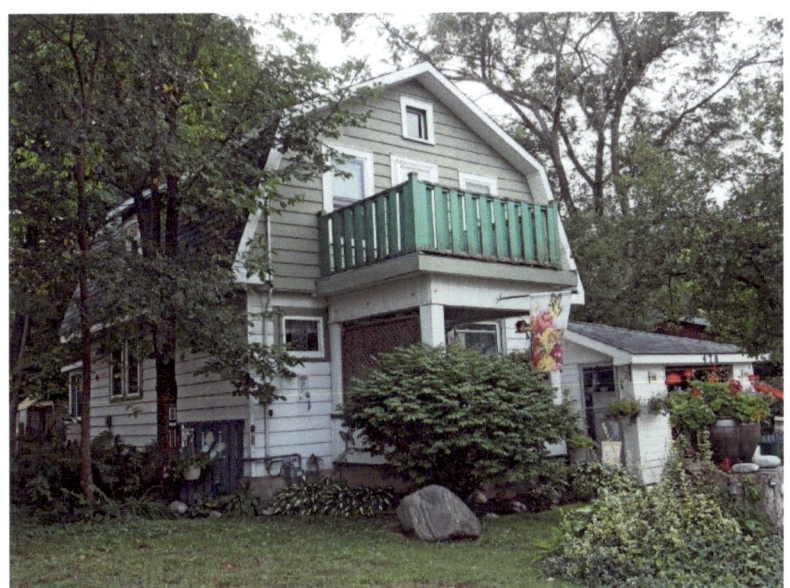

478 Midland Avenue – Neo-colonial – gambrel roof, second floor balcony

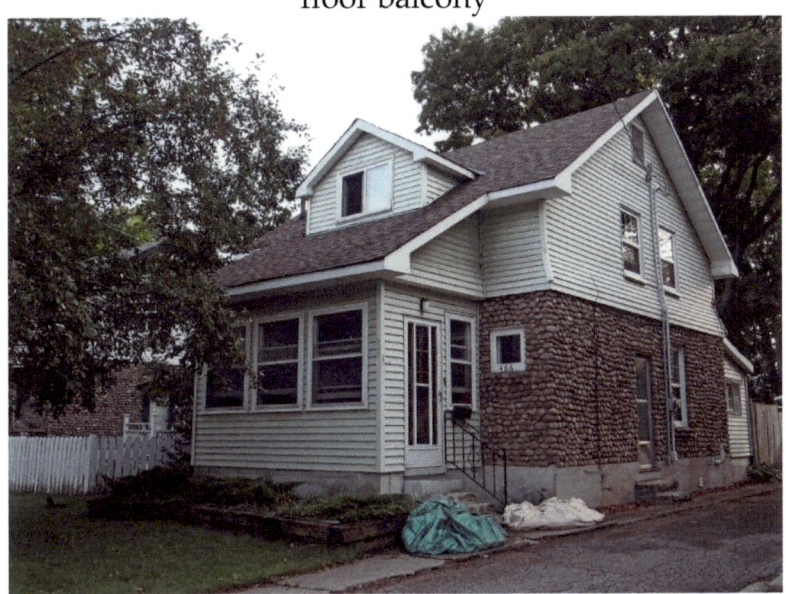

486 Midland Avenue – 1930 – 2½ storeys tall with a full below ground basement; exterior is clapboard, plain field stone and a poured concrete foundation; medium gable roof with gable dormer; closed porch covered with clap board

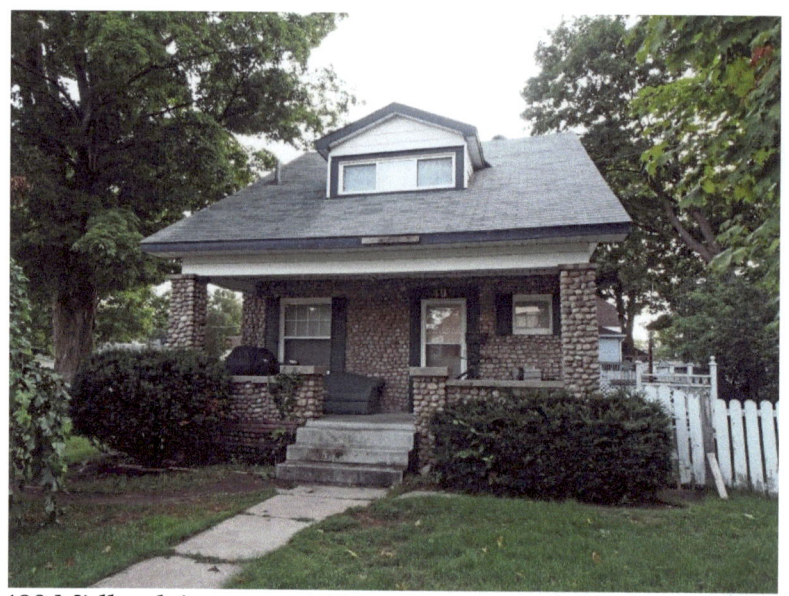

490 Midland Avenue – 1930 – 1½ storeys, full below ground basement; medium gable roof with gable dormer; exterior finished with field stone; 8-over-1 window panes; open porch with closed railings and stone piers

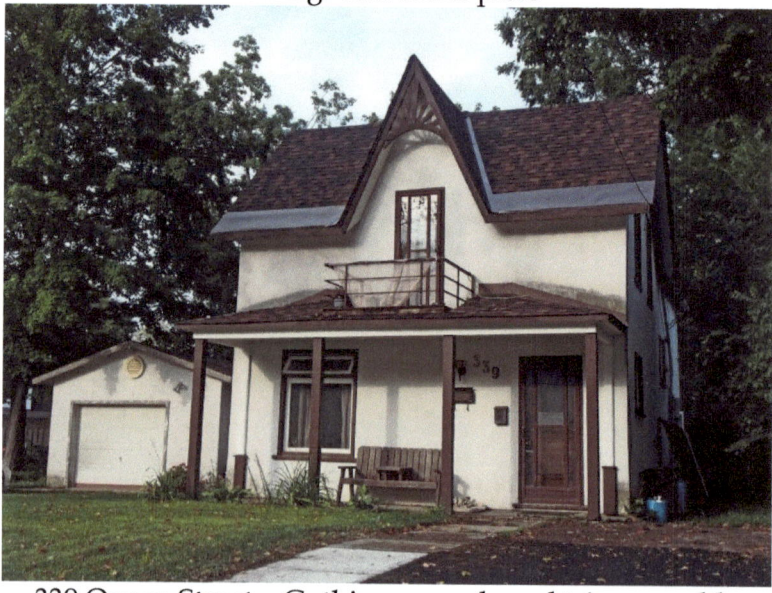

339 Queen Street – Gothic – verge board trim on gable

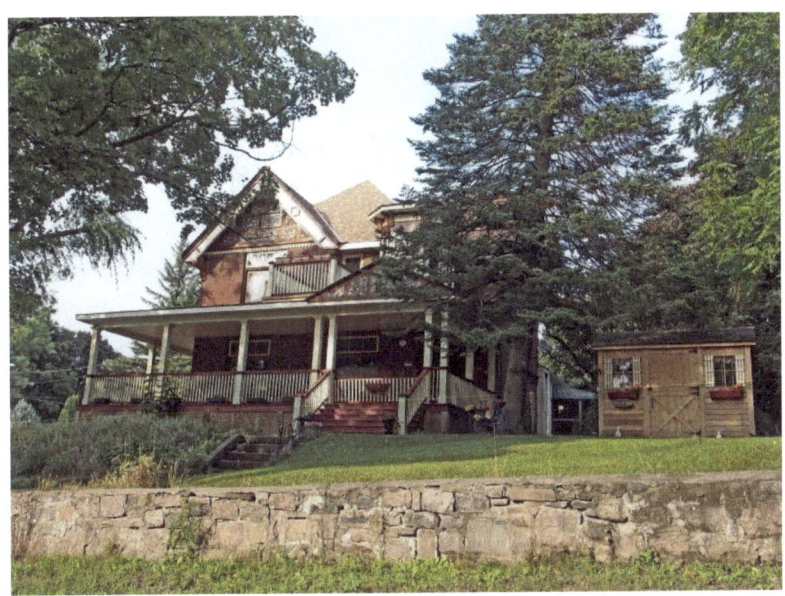

251 Queen Street – 1875 - Queen Anne Revival style - large wrap-around veranda, tower, ornate brackets, brick detailing on chimney, multiple roof lines, multi-paned art glass and numerous dormers and gables; decorative solid bargeboard; crushed glass façades beneath the gables; exposed purlins along the roof edges; eyebrow windows, etched glass, stained glass and diamond-shaped decorative paned windows; original stone retaining wall along both Queen Street and Dominion Avenue

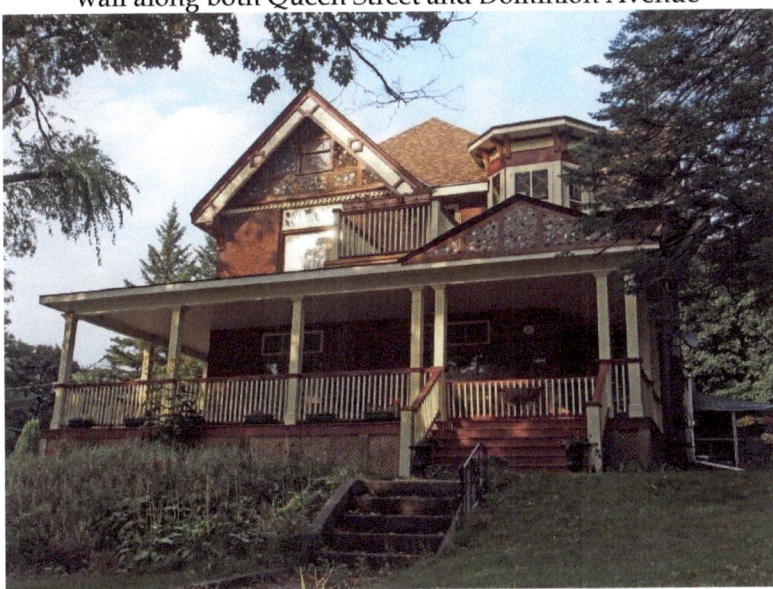

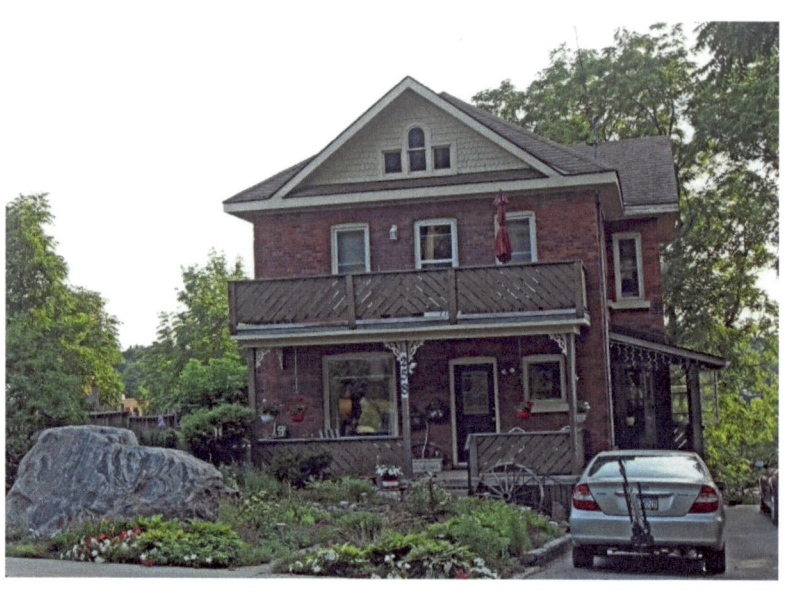

258 Queen Street – 1900 - Georgian style – 2½ storey house with full below ground basement; exterior is brick with wood shingles on gable; pyramidal roof offset with two gables; Palladian window with decorative trim in gable; wooden veranda with posts, a closed railing and decorative supports at the roof; upper storey balcony with closed railing; stained glass window beside doorway and crescent-shaped window and cedar shakes on the front gable

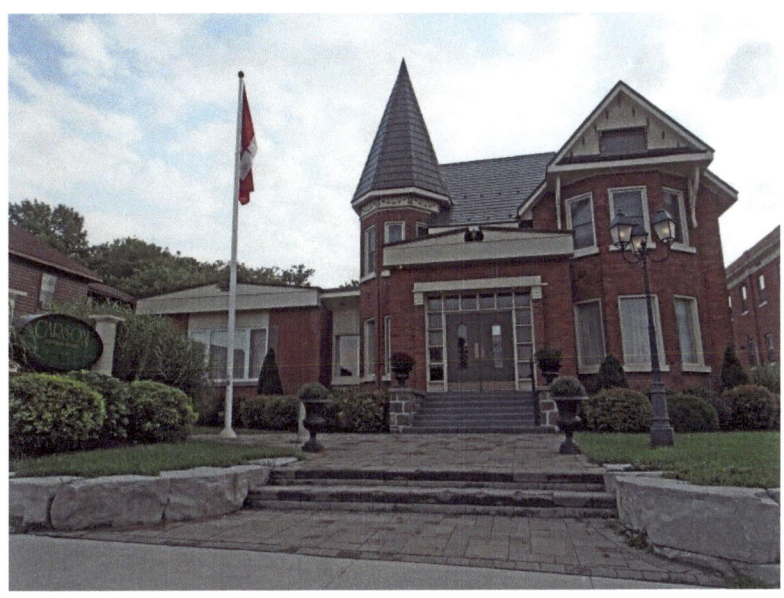

290 First Street – Carson Funeral Home since 1878 – turret

The Lynn-Carson Funeral Home's present location was formerly the residence of Mr. J.R. Morrow, one of the area's first funeral directors. Mr. Morrow operated a funeral business from the back of his furniture store at 282 King Street, at a time when furniture and caskets were seen as related products. Most funerals were conducted in the home of the deceased, or from the church. Morrow purchased the combined furniture-casket store in 1883 from Mr. C.W. Laing, who had founded the store in 1878. When Morrow sold the business to Alexander Barrie in 1912, he purchased the present location of the Lynn-Carson Funeral Home as his residence.

Mr. Barrie then branched out and began Midland's first ambulance during the early years of the Great War. In the 1930s, St. Andrew's Hospital took over the operation.

During the Depression in the 1930s, people began living in more urbanized flats and apartments, creating a need for funeral visitation space. At this time Alex Barrie purchased J.R. Morrow's home on First St. and converted it into a funeral home. In 1961, the chapel was added.

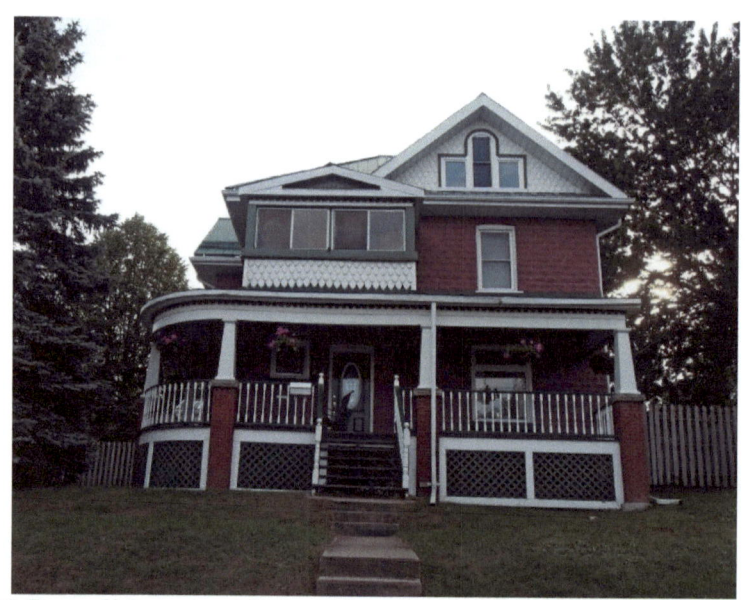

322 Russell Street – 1885 – Edwardian - 2½ storeys; exterior is painted, even, cut course stone and terra cotta; closed-in upper storey balcony; pyramidal roof; Palladian window in both gables; stained glass window next to door; wraparound veranda with open railing, brick supports, and wood piers

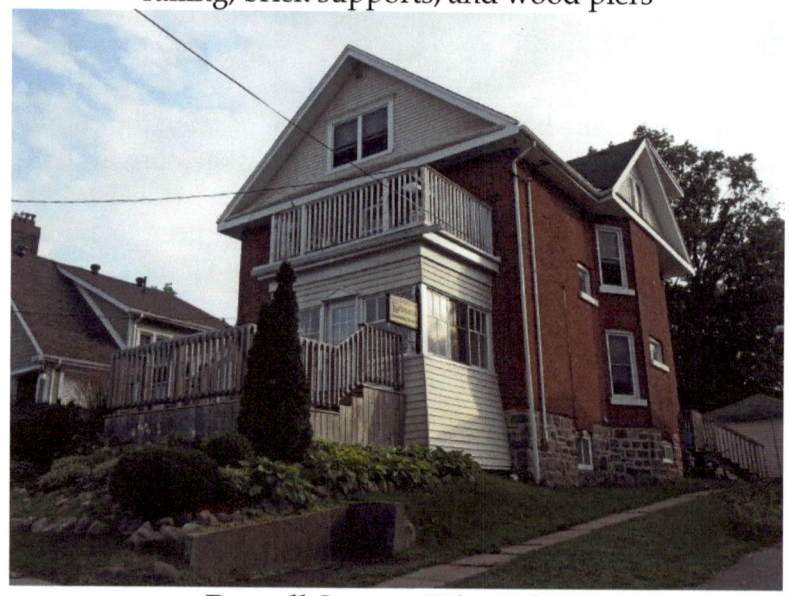

Russell Street - Edwardian

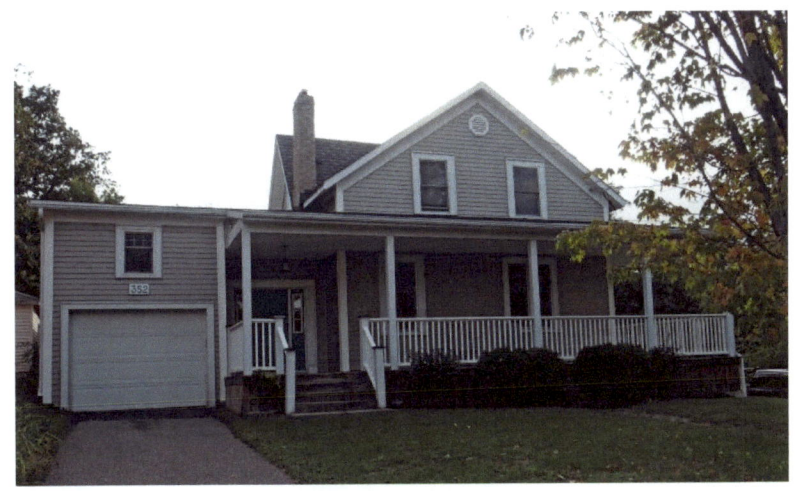

Yonge Street

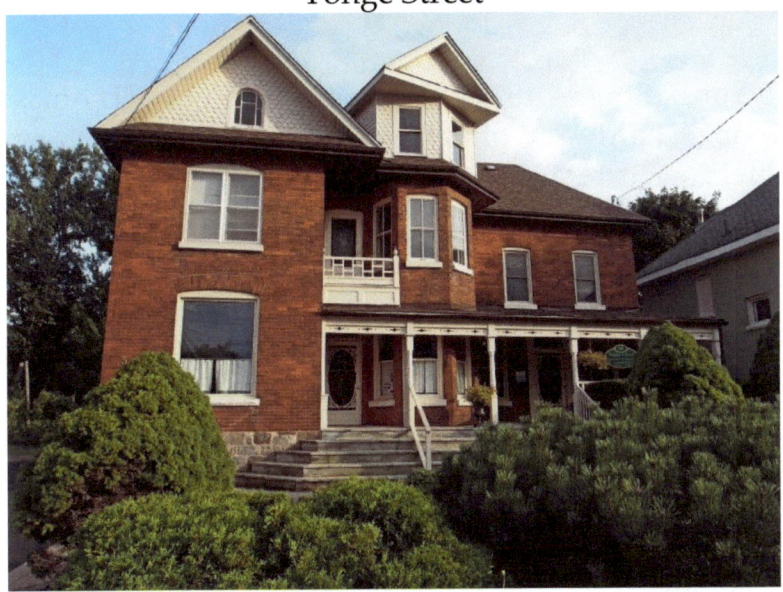

537 Yonge Street – 1870 – 2½ storeys; exterior is wood shingles, even course cut stone, stretcher brick, and terra cotta; upper storey balcony; medium hipped roof with an offset gable and bay dormer with a gable pediment for the roof; brick voussoirs; semi-elliptical window in the gable; stained glass window above the window on the front left side; single light transom; open veranda with open railing, wood supports, decorative columns, and decorative trim on roof

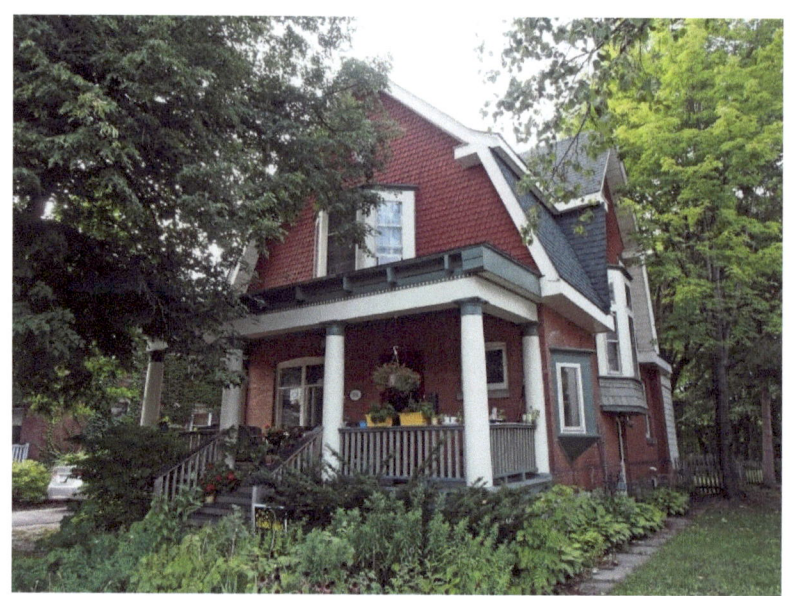

556 Yonge Street – 1874 - The Campbell House (Thomas J. Campbell, hardware, plumbing and heating store) - hipped gambrel roof; exterior is brick with shingle in the upper gable; bay windows; open veranda with plain pillars for support

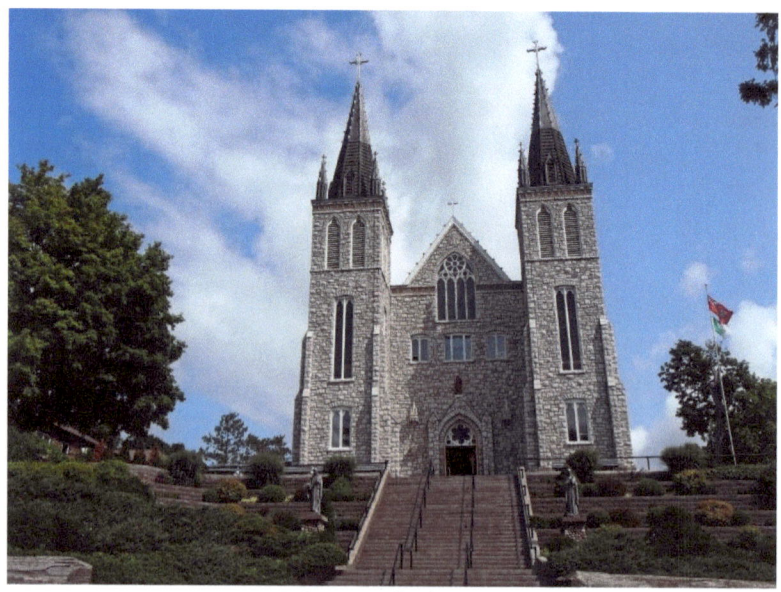

Martyrs' Shrine

Architectural Terms

Banding: Different materials, colors or textures used in horizontal bands along a wall. Example: 307 Third Street, Page 11	
Bay Window: A window that projects out from a wall, in a semicircular, rectangular, or polygonal design. Used frequently in Gothic and Victorian designs. Example: 423 Hugel Avenue, Page 42	
Brackets: a decorative or weight-bearing structural element which forms a right angle with one side against a wall and the other under a projecting surface such as an eave or roof. Example: 657 Hugel Avenue, Page 30	
Buttress: a masonry structure built against or projecting from a wall which serves to support or reinforce the wall. In Canadian architecture, they are sometimes used for decoration. Example: 589 Hugel Avenue, Page 37	

Capital: The uppermost finish or decoration on a column. An Ionic column has a small base, a thin elegant shaft, and a capital composed of volutes which are carved whirls or twists that take the form of a scroll. Example: 695 Dominion Avenue, Page 29 A Doric column is characterized by a plain column with no base, a shaft with twenty flutings, and a simple capital with a simple entablature. Example: 421 Midland Avenue, Page 51	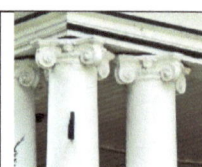 Ionic 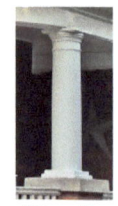 Doric
Cobblestone architecture: Refers to the use of cobblestones embedded in mortar as a method for erecting walls on houses and commercial buildings. Example: Fourth Street, Page 16	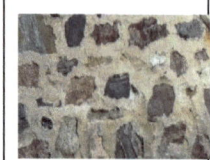
Dichromatic brickwork: the use of two colours of brick, tile or slate to decorate a façade. Example: 307 Third Street, Page 11	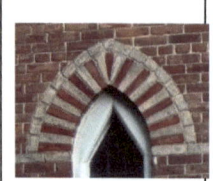
Dormer: (French for "sleep") a gable end window that pierces through the plane of a sloping roof surface to create usable space in the top floor or attic of a building by adding headroom. Example: 86 Fourth Street, Page 14	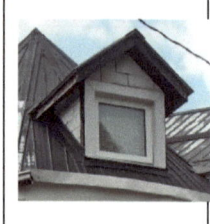

Frontispiece: a portion of the façade of a building, usually a centred doorway that is slightly raised from the rest of the building, usually has extensive ornamentation. Frontispieces are usually Classical in design with white columned porches. Example: 526 Hugel Avenue, Page 40	
Gable: the triangular portion of a wall between the edges of a sloping roof. Example: 318 Third Street, Page 13	
Gambrel Roof: a symmetrical two-sided roof with two slopes on each side; the upper slope is positioned at a shallow angle, while the lower slope is steep. It is similar to a mansard roof, but a gambrel has vertical gable ends instead of being hipped at the four corners of the building. Example: 129 Fifth Street, Page 20	
Hipped Roof: a roof where all sides slope downwards to the walls with no gables. Example: 659 Dominion Avenue, Page 28	
Keystones: is the central stone that locks all the stones into position, allowing the arch to bear weight. A keystone is often enlarged and embellished. Example: 526 Hugel Avenue, Page 40	

Lancet Window: a tall, narrow window with a pointed arch at its top. Example: 307 Third Street, Page 11	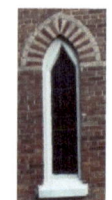
Muntin: When a window unit has more than one pane, the material that separates the panes is called the muntin. The larger, more decorative separations are called mullions. In stained glass windows, each piece of colored glass is held in place by a muntin. These were traditionally made of iron. Example: 589 Hugel Avenue, Page 37	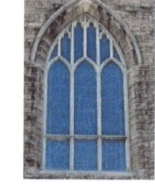
Oriel Window - These small areas were originally set into walls and galleries for the purpose of private prayer. Over time, any projecting window or area on an upper floor was called an oriel. Example: 695 Dominion Avenue, Page 29	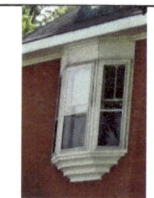
Palladian Window: a large window that is divided into three sections with the centre section larger than the two side sections and usually arched. Example: Hugel Avenue, Page 31	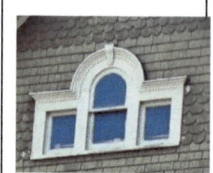
Pediment: a triangular section above the door or portico, usually supported by columns. The inside of the triangle is called the tympanum. Example: 695 Dominion Avenue, Page 29	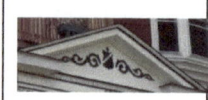

Portal: is an opening in a wall of a building, gate or fortification, especially a grand entrance to an important structure. Example: 589 Hugel Avenue, Page 37	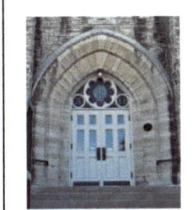
The **quatrefoil** is a type of decorative framework consisting of a symmetrical shape which forms the outline of four partially overlapping circles of the same diameter. The word quatrefoil comes from Latin and means "four leaves". Example: 589 Hugel Avenue, Page 37	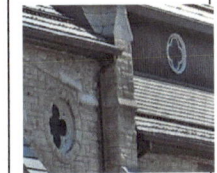
Quoin: masonry blocks at the corner of a wall, often a decorative feature, usually larger or of a different colour than the rest of the wall. Example: Hugel Avenue, Page 33	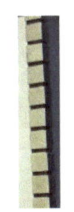
Rose Window: a circular window with ornamental tracery radiating from the centre. Example: 589 Hugel Avenue, Page 39	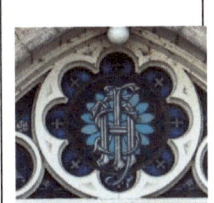
Sidelight: a vertical window that flanks a door, and is often used to emphasize the importance of a primary entrance. Example: 632 Hugel Avenue, Page 32	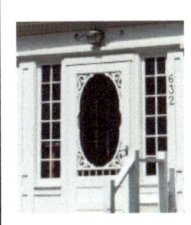

Tower: A circular, square, or octagonal vertical structure higher than the surrounding structure that is usually part of an existing building and is created either for extra defense or for a specific purpose such as a clock or a bell tower. Example: 589 Hugel Avenue, Page 37	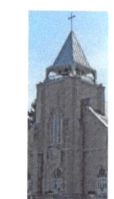
Transom Window: the light above the doorway, also called a fanlight. Example: 613 Dominion Avenue, Page 26	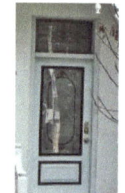
Turret: a small tower that projects from the wall of a building. Example: 290 First Street, Page 56	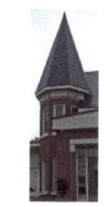
Verge board and Finial: also called bargeboards – hang from the projecting end of a roof and are often elaborately carved and ornamented. **Finial:** ornament added to the top of a gable, pinnacle, canopy or spire – a Gothic element. Example: 294 Third Street, Page 12	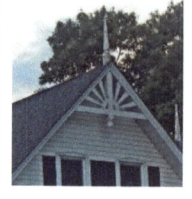

Building Styles

Edwardian, 1900-1930 – This style bridges the ornate and elaborate styles of the Victorian era and the simplified styles of the 20th century. Balanced facades, simple roof lines, dormer windows, large front porches, and smooth brick surfaces are its characteristics. Example: 644 Hugel Avenue, Page 34	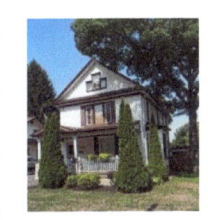
Georgian, before 1860 – This style began with the British King Georges in the 18th century. These buildings have balanced facades around a central door, medium-pitched gable roofs, and small paned windows. Example: 258 Queen Street, Page 55	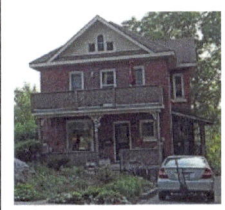
Gothic Revival, 1830-1890 – These decorative buildings have sharply-pitched gables with highly detailed verge boards, pointed-arch window openings, and dichromatic brickwork. It is a common style in Ontario. Example: 307 Third Street, Page 11	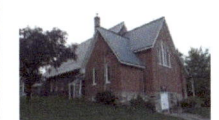
Neo-colonial architecture seeks to revive elements of architectural style of American colonial architecture of the period around the Revolutionary War which drew strongly from Georgian architecture of Great Britain. Structures are typically two stories, have a symmetrical front facade with elaborate front doorways, often with decorative crown pediments, fanlights, and sidelights, symmetrical windows flanking the front entrance. Example: 129 Fifth Street, Page 20	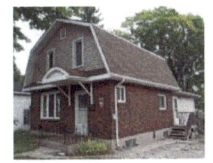

Queen Anne, 1885-1900 – This style is distinguished by an irregular outline featuring a combination of an offset tower, broad gables, projecting two-storey bays, verandahs, multi-sloped roofs, and tall, decorative chimneys. A mixture of brick and wood is common. Windows often have one large single-paned bottom sash and small panes in the upper sash. Example: 251 Queen Street, Page 54	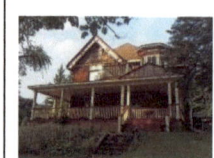
Romanesque Revival, 1880-1910 – This style hearkens back to medieval architecture of the 11th and 12th centuries with a heavy appearance, blocky towers and rounded arches. Example: 539 Hugel Avenue, Page 38	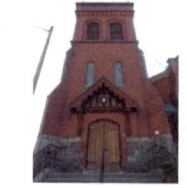
Vernacular/Traditional Mode 1638 - 1950 Influenced but not defined by a particular style, vernacular buildings are made from easily available materials and exhibit local design characteristics. Example: 620 Hugel Avenue, Page 34	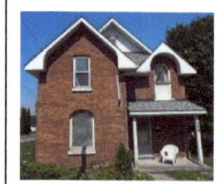
Victorian - In Ontario, a Victorian style building can be seen as any building built between 1840 and 1900 that doesn't fit into any of the other categories. It encompasses a large group of buildings constructed in brick, stone, and timber, using an eclectic mixture of Classical and Gothic motifs. Example: 318 Third Street, Page 13	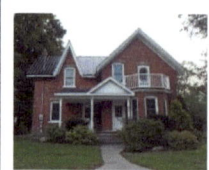

www.ingramcontent.com/pod-product-compliance
Lightning Source LLC
Chambersburg PA
CBHW040811200526
45159CB00022B/226